MODERN LEGAL STUDIES

KT-148-785

EXCLUSION CLAUSES
IN CONTRACTS

General Editor of the Series
Professor J.P.W.B. McAuslan

Editorial Board
Professor W.R. Cornish
Professor T.C. Daintith
R.P. Grime
Professor J.D. McClean
Professor C. Palley

AUSTRALIA
The Law Book Company Ltd.
Sydney : Melbourne : Brisbane

CANADA AND U.S.A.
The Carswell Company Ltd.
Agincourt, Ontario

INDIA
N.M. Tripathi Private Ltd.
Bombay
and
Eastern Law House Private Ltd.
Calcutta

M.P.P. House
Bangalore

ISRAEL
Steimatzky's Agency Ltd.
Jerusalem : Tel Aviv : Haifa

MALAYSIA : SINGAPORE : BRUNEI
Malayan Law Journal (Pte.) Ltd.
Singapore

NEW ZEALAND
Sweet & Maxwell (N.Z.) Ltd.
Wellington

PAKISTAN
Pakistan Law House
Karachi

MODERN LEGAL STUDIES

EXCLUSION CLAUSES IN CONTRACTS

by

DAVID YATES, M.A. (Oxon.)

Senior Lecturer in Law
at the University of Manchester

LONDON
SWEET & MAXWELL
1978

Published in 1978 by
Sweet & Maxwell Limited of
11 New Fetter Lane, London.
Photoset by Red Lion Setters, London.
Printed in Great Britain by
Fletcher & Son Ltd., Norwich

ISBN Hardback 0 421 240380 X
Paperback 0 421 240407

PREFACE

In 1964 Professor Coote published a seminal work entitled *Exception Clauses*. It would be presumptious to contemplate this work becoming, in any sense, a substitute for that work which is still, notwithstanding the passage of 13 years since its publication, compulsory reading for any student of the subject. The present writer's debt to Professor Coote's work is great and no doubt obvious. However, case law and statute have developed quite markedly since 1964, sometimes along the lines suggested by Professor Coote, sometimes not. It was thought useful to produce, at this time, a commentary on the law as it appears at present, in a form (one hopes) easily read and digested by undergraduate students, and to suggest in what ways the law might be modified to meet current commercial and consumer needs.

This leads on to the second purpose of this book. The writer has undertaken empirical research amongst the business and consumer communities and was struck first, by the apparent influence the consumer interest now carries with both the legislature and the judiciary and secondly, by the inadequacy of the law, in some quarters of the business community quite strongly felt, to provide a solution to the commercial problems of commercial men. It therefore seemed appropriate to fit this information, much of which was given with great enthusiasm by legal departments of the various business interests consulted, into the context of a legal framework. This is, however, a technical subject presented in a relatively technical way. Nevertheless, the writer believes that the lawyer should, in operating a system of rules, more especially highly technical ones, be aware of the problems of the community which this system is trying to serve. Only then will sympathetic understanding and rational development be achieved.

After this work had been written, the Unfair Contract Terms Bill began its slow progress through Parliament. It was hoped that by the time the manuscript was ready for publication the legislature would have decided, one way or the other, on the fate of this Bill, but this was not to be. Instead I was faced with the somewhat unsatisfactory position, from the reader's point of view, of legislation imminent but not enacted. Consequently I wrote this book in the firm and settled belief that the Bill would become law by the end of the year and made my comments in the light of the text available at the time of writing. It seemed unlikely that much substantial change would take place in the proposed provisions between then and the receipt of the Royal Assent and it was therefore hoped that these first thoughts would help the reader to understand the possible significance for the future of the interaction between the common law rules and the new statutory provisions. After receiving the proofs of this work, the Bill received the Royal Assent and, with the co-operation of the publishers, it was possible to make suitable ammendments to the text so as to reflect what is now the common law as modified by the new legislation.

Many people have assisted me in the preparation of the research for Chapter 1 and most of them for various reasons (but not, I hope, because I have misrepresented their views) refuse to be named. I would like to express my particular thanks, however, to Messrs. R. Leslie, P. Tout, D. Walker and G. Underhill for their assistance. My thanks also to Mrs. Sheila Levitt, for turning an almost indecipherable manuscript into a neat and readable typescript, to my secretary Mrs. Beth Lambert, for her assistance with the survey material, and finally to my wife Carolyn, for her unfailing help, advice and timely criticism throughout the writing of this book. Any deficiencies which remain are entirely mine.

The law is as stated on December 1, 1977.

Dalton Hall,
University of Manchester   David Yates

CONTENTS

OTHER BOOKS IN THE SERIES:

TABLE OF CASES

TABLE OF STATUTES

Chapter 1

EXCLUSION CLAUSES IN CONTEXT

A. *Standard Form Contracts*

1. *General*

During the *laissez-faire* era of the early nineteenth century, exemption clauses were tolerated, if not actually encouraged, under the all-pervading doctrine of freedom of contract. By exclusion clause here is meant, as a general guide, any term in a contract restricting a remedy or a liability arising out of a breach of a contractual obligation. There are other types of exclusion clauses, and these are discussed later in this Chapter, but such a statement will serve for our present purposes. The demands of the industrial revolution, gathering momentum as it did during the middle years of the last century, created mass production using the new technology that would produce limitless numbers of standard articles by standardised processes. Such production methods required similarly standardised mass produced contracts and this, in turn, resulted in mass produced exclusion clauses. These new contracts are referred to as being, for obvious reasons, standard-form.[1]

A standard-form contract, once its contents have been formulated by a business firm, is used in every bargain dealing with the same product or service with every client or customer. The individuality of the parties becomes irrelevant. Once the usefulness of these contracts was discovered and perfected in the transport, insurance and banking businesses, their use spread into all other fields of large scale enterprise, such as national and international trade, supplies by the statutory undertakers, consumer sales and credit agreements.

In so far as the reduction of production and distribution costs which such agreements achieve is reflected in reduced prices, society as a whole may ultimately benefit from the use of standard-form contracts. Their use has, however, another aspect, which has become increasingly important. Standard-form contracts are typically used by enterprises with strong bargaining power. The weaker party, in need of the goods or services, is frequently not in a position to shop around for better terms, either because the supplier has a monopoly (such as the statutory undertakers supplying gas, water, electricity, etc.), or because all competitors use the same clause (for example all architects designing family houses will use the RIBA Standard Conditions of Engagement). The "consumer's" contractual intention is but a subjection, more or less voluntarily, to terms dictated by the stronger party, terms whose consequences are often understood only in a vague way, if at all. Thus standard-form contracts are frequently contracts of adhesion; they are "take-it-or-leave-it" terms.[2]

As well as being a weapon of consumer oppression, however, the standard form contract is also a tool of commercial convenience. A business that deals with many customers or suppliers or holders of dealer franchises does not ordinarily find it feasible either to negotiate with, or evaluate the business acumen and sincerity of the other party to any degree. Further, if the dealing is anticipated to extend over a long period, changes of personnel, company or trading policy, or the market, may make it difficult to predict how the other party is likely to behave in the future. It is thus more convenient to require adhesion to a contract that commits a business, legally, to performance far less than it is expected to render, and to qualify promises by conditions that will not be insisted upon unless good business relations break down.

This will not necessarily involve the imposition of harsh terms as a result of superior bargaining power. The business may be quite competitive but the parties simply wish to eliminate, so far as possible, the legal hazard. By utilising a standard form of agreement, time spent negotiating separate agreements is saved and, unless relations between the parties turn sour, their legal agreement need not be looked at again, aside from minor alterations to price or specification clauses, for many months or even, on occasions, years.

The uniformity of terms of contracts typically recurring in a business enterprise is an important factor in the exact calculation of risks. Risks which are difficult to calculate can be excluded altogether. Unforeseeable contingencies affecting performance, such as strikes, fire, unavailability of raw materials such as oil or coal, can be taken care of.[3] The standard exclusion clauses in insurance policies are a striking illustration of successful attempts on the part of business enterprises to select and control risks assumed under a contract.[4] The insurance community, indeed, brought risk control to new heights of refinement, by first realising the full importance of "juridical risk," the danger that a court may be swayed by "irrational factors" to decide against a powerful defendant. This was soon adopted by other members of the business community. So, for example, the desire to avoid juridical risks has been a motivating factor in the use of arbitration clauses in international trade agreements.

However, our economy reached a point at which, notwithstanding certain advantages for businessmen *inter se*, the possibility of contracts freely negotiated securing a fair market equilibrium became an illusion. As one writer has expressed it[5]: "*Liberté* had devoured *égalité* and *fraternité* was succeeded by the fierce competition of industrial giants." The exclusion clause in the standard form contract became a potent weapon for the exploitation of economic power. The courts and the legal system still hung on to the old ideas of freedom of contract. The judges continued to support the "commercial" interest,[6] the pure profit-interests of industry, the entrepreneur and later the corporations, and thus a conflict was created with the socio-political interests of capital as a whole. The further development and, in some cases (for example the field of labour relations) the survival of the socio-political system required a new policy. It created in the field of the law of contract the displacement of the "commercial" interest by the "consumer" interest, both in the courts and in parliament, to mitigate the consequences of large-scale private businesses. The consequence was a new approach to industry and commerce which, through its standard form contracts, could no longer be allowed to misuse its bargaining power, superior resources and commercial know-how to impose standardised, unfair and oppressive terms on consumers. As Professor Flemming has put it[7]: "Disclaimers belong to the era of free enterprise, the rejection of disclaimers to the era of social welfare."

2. *Legislative Proposals*

The Unfair Contract Terms Act 1977, makes reference, in section 3(1), to a party to a contract dealing with the other party on "the other's written standard terms of business." The object of the section is to prevent a party in breach of, *inter alia*, a standard form contract from relying on an exclusion clause unless he has established that the clause satisfies the statutory requirement of "reasonableness." The concept of reasonableness under the Act is discussed in Chapter 3, and the operation of section 3(1) in Chapter 4. However, it is worth mentioning that the Act makes no attempt to define what is meant by "written standard terms of business" and so there are likely to be some difficult decisions to be made as to when the contract is, or is not, "standard form." If one of the parties is dealing as a consumer (see Chap. 3) then the question of whether or not the document is standard form becomes irrelevant, since all contracts in which one of the parties deals as a consumer are brought within section 3. However, if both parties are commercial men, it may be a very difficult question to decide how frequently a set of terms need to be used before they become "standard" or to what extent express modifications or striking out of certain terms will prevent a document being regarded as standard form for the purposes of the section.

Lord Denning M.R. has recently expressed his views on standard form contracts and, in some measure, anticipated the enactment of the Act, in *Levison* v. *Patent Steam Carpet Cleaning Co. Ltd.*[8] He said:

"In such circumstances [where a standard form agreement is the means of imposing onerous conditions on consumers] ... the Law Commission in 1975 recommended that a term which exempts the stronger party from his ordinary common law liability should not be given effect except when it is reasonable ... and there is a bill now before Parliament which gives effect to the test of reasonableness. This is a gratifying piece of law reform: but I do not think we need wait for that bill to be passed into law. You never know what may happen to a bill."

Lord Denning M.R. then produced his own concept of reasonableness, derived from the common law, to invalidate the clause in that case.

Perhaps the best guidance, although of little practical help, being more in the nature of an observation than a definition, of how the courts are likely to interpret the "standard terms of business" provision of section 3(1), is to be found in the judgment of Lord Diplock in *Instone* v. *A. Schroeder Music Publishing Co. Ltd.*[9] He said:

"This [standard form contract] is of comparatively modern origin. It is the result of the concentration of particular kinds of business in relatively few hands ... The terms ... have not been the subject of negotiation between the parties to it, or approved by any organisation representing the interests of the weaker party. They have been dictated by that party whose bargaining power, either exercised alone or in conjunction with others providing similar goods or services, enables him to say: 'If you want these goods or services at all, these are the only terms on which they are obtainable. Take it or leave it.'."

However, the protection of the consumer interest must not be so vigorous as to inhibit the legitimate expectation of businessmen, contracting on an equal footing. As will be illustrated throughout the rest of this work, we have so far reached the stage of recognising both the commercial interest and the consumer interest in our recent law-making but the latter has tended to be promoted at the expense of the former. What the law should be striving at is the alignment of desirable economic efficiency with the necessary protection of the individual. A technological society founded on capitalism must recognise and understand the normative power given to the economic sector.[10] It demands not a social, but an economic contract. Society must be aware of the demands of the economic machine for efficiency, productivity and profit which it has itself created; in formulating its protections against those who abuse their bargaining strength society must not sacrifice the rational administration of the economy. To recognise, therefore, the existence of the consumer interest, possibly at odds with the commercial interest, is not, alone, sophisticated enough to achieve this end.

In particular, with reference to exclusion clauses, it is damaging to regulate their operation by reference to which of these two interests, commercial or consumer, needs the greatest protection unless, at the same time, the individual clause is examined in the context of the contract as a whole. There is no such thing as an exclusion clause in the abstract. It only makes sense in the context of the other terms and obligations of the contract. If the consumer interest needs protection against the commercial interest this can best be achieved, as will be shown later, not by trying to regulate a particular clause or clauses, but by regulating the entire legal relationship.

B. *Economic Justification*[11]

Any commercial contract is ultimately an attempt by resource owners to combine their respective resources for the production of profit. There is a variety of contractual arrangements under which this is done and there are at least two reasons why the business community requires these different types of contractual arrangements. First, is the existence of natural risk, defined here as the contribution made by nature or the state of the world to the variance of the product value. Given a variable range of possible total income from the project for the contracting parties, different contractual arrangements may allow different distributions of income variances among the contracting parties. Assuming an individual will seek to avoid a risk if the cost of doing so is less than the gain from the risk averted, he will do so in one of three ways. First, he may search for information about the future (for example by using actuarial assessment) but this may not be available, even at infinitely high cost. Secondly, he may choose less risky options when investing (for instance, by checking the credit rating of the other party in advance, or simply diversifying his commercial activities in the exploitation of his assets). Thirdly, he may select arrangements by which his burden of risk can be dispersed to other individuals. This can be achieved, of course, by insurance, or it can be achieved by exclusion clauses.

A second reason for the existence of different contractual arrangements lies in the different transaction costs that are associated with them. Transaction costs are the costs of negotiating and enforcing the stipulations of the contract and will depend upon such factors as the number of parties, changes in prices, specification and so on. Transaction costs differ because physical attributes of input-output differ, because institutional arrangements differ and because different sets of stipulations require varying efforts in enforcement and negotiation. So, the choice, then of contractual arrangement is made so as to maximise the gain from risk dispersion, subject to the constraint of transaction cost.

The current policy of protecting the consumer interest involves the view that the enterprise causing the damage is the best distributor of loss, either by distributing the loss among its consumers or clients through prices or by distributing the loss among the group of those causing similar damage, through insurance. Such an approach bans, or at least actively discourages, risk aversion by means of exclusion clauses altogether. In economic terms such an approach is a necessary first step in evaluating the need for selective intervention in this field. If one assumes that the true cost of damage cannot be properly evaluated in the market place unless the agent producing it is made responsible for the damage,[12] then a ban on exclusion clauses is the first step in analysing the extent to which it is necessary to inhibit commercial operations, as against the free play of self interest, in order to provide that a proper proportion of the country's resources is made available to compensate injured parties.

This, of course, ignores two difficulties. First, the wrong animal may be caged. It is not the clause, but the whole contractual arrangement, that disperses risk. A skilled draftsman can always evade a ban on exemption clauses by expressing a contract in positive and limited form instead of in general terms, limited by specific exemptions. Secondly, in the long run it is unlikely to have any impact on the overall allocation of resources within the capitalist structure. If manufacturers cannot contract out of liability for defects in their goods when they sell direct to the public, but can if they sell to retailers or wholesalers, there are likely to be more wholesalers and retailers than if such contracting out were permitted, since they represent a better market for the manufacturer than direct dealings with the public. Regardless, therefore, of the resources available to compensate the consumer for his defective product, he will have to pay more for his goods to cover profit for the "middlemen" than perhaps he would if he purchased direct from the manufacturer.

C. *Use of Exclusion Clauses in Commercial Planning — The Practical Experience*

Businessmen utilise legal processes, notably the law of contract, to plan certain aspects of their commercial dealings. Summers[13] has characterised this as "the grievance remedial technique" and "the private arranging technique." The grievance remedial technique is the resort to legal remedies when the commercial relationship breaks down. So, this would include repudiation of the contract, actions for damages, arbitrations and out-of-court settlements. The private arranging technique involves the use of the contract by the parties to regulate their relationship and plan what is to happen in the future. The parties will, therefore, in a contract of sale, plan such matters as the goods, the price, the quantities, the dates and manner of carriage and delivery and so on. They may also provide for certain contingencies and for who is to carry the risk or the cost should some subsequent event make performance of the primary obligations impossible, difficult or different, for example because raw materials become unavailable, or more costly, or because of a strike or a fire. If the contract then specifies remedies that are to arise should something go wrong with their relationship, for example an arbitration clause, or a liquidated damages clause, then, of course, the grievance remedial technique and the private arranging technique merge.

Exclusion clauses will be incorporated into contracts by businessmen as part of the private arranging technique although they will frequently have their operation when resort is had to the grievance remedial technique. So, for example, a provision that a carrier shall not be liable for loss from a consignment unless he is advised of the loss in writing within seven days from the date of delivery has the effect of restricting liability arising out of a breach of any obligation of the contract. It is part of the private arranging technique in that it attempts to anticipate a particular set of circumstances that may arise in the future and to plan for them, but it is also part of the procedure for securing grievance remedies. A more complex example is that found in *Anglo-Continental Holidays Ltd.* v. *Typaldos Lines (London) Ltd.*[14] In that case the defendants, who were travel agents, agreed to book for the plaintiffs, who were also travel agents, cruises on a named ship following a fixed itinerary. The agreement was subject to a clause which provided that the vessels, sailing dates and itineraries were "subject to change without prior notice." Relying on this clause, the defendants offered the plaintiffs cruises on a different ship following a different itinerary; the substituted vessel was inferior to the original named ship and the plaintiffs regarded the substituted itinerary as also inferior.

Lord Denning M.R., on the assumption that the clause formed part of the contract, appeared to regard it as an exclusion clause, holding that the defendants could not rely on a clause of this kind so as to alter what the parties had actually agreed. On this view, therefore, in incorporating the clause the parties had in view the remedy of grievances. Russell L.J., however, said that it was not an exemption clause: "It is a clause under which the actual contractual liability may be defined, and not one which will excuse from the actual contractual liability ... I prefer to state it as being a matter of construction of a general clause, and the propounder of that clause cannot be enabled thereby to alter the substance of the arrangement."[15] Russell L.J., then, appears to regard the clause as inserted as part of the private arranging technique although, of course, its operation clearly affects available remedies.

Such an analysis is not especially helpful in determining the legal consequences of exclusion clauses. As an objective analysis it is simply a method rather less reliable than those other tests used in the law of contract for ascertaining contractual intention. As a subjective analysis, however, it is useful. Assuming the parties are prepared to provide the necessary information as to their commercial and contractual intentions, it assists in determining to what extent, if at all, businessmen "use" contract law in general, and exclusion clauses in particular, in planning their commercial transactions. If they do not it may be because the legal rules which have been developed for the resolution of disputes in this area do not provide satisfactory remedies, or the consequences attached by the law to particular contractual terms do not adequately fulfil the parties' expectations.

Very little empirical research has been carried out into the attitude of businessmen towards contractual procedures in the conduct of their business affairs. In the U.S.A. Macaulay [16] carried out research amongst 48 companies and six law firms in Wisconsin. He described contract as involving "two distinct elements: (a) rational planning of the transaction with careful provision for as many future contingencies as can be foreseen, and (b) the existence or use of actual or potential legal sanctions to induce performance of the exchange or to compensate for non-performance." He identified four types of issue which might be planned for — description of the primary obligations, contingencies, defective performances and legal sanctions. Exclusion clauses, of course, may be key devices in planning for all of these. Macaulay concluded that while many business exchanges will involve a high degree of planning about each category, equally many at least "reflect no planning or only a minimal amount of it, especially concerning legal sanctions and the effect of defective performance." He found very little use of "contractual practices" in the later adjustment of relationships, though there was some evidence of tacit reliance on contractual rights, and very little use of formal dispute-settlement procedures available through the courts.

The most important published research on the approach of English businessmen to the use of contractual practices is that carried out by Beale and Dugdale in Bristol in 1973 and 1974.[17] Their conclusions were similar to Macaulay's. Businessmen tended to eschew contractual remedies as being too inflexible, and lawyers as being unsympathetic to the problems of businessmen. There was a similar reluctance to use the law in planning operations, save that if the risk justified it, there would be careful planning, hard bargaining and especially careful legal drafting. Macaulay's research tended to support this finding. It prompted the present writer to attempt to ascertain to what extent the use of exclusion clauses in contracts supported this proposition.

The presence of an exclusion clause indicates either the presence of a risk which one party wishes to transfer to the other, or it indicates a very precise attempt to define the obligations the promisor is undertaking. In both cases it shows a high level of planning and a close regard to the private arranging technique, at least in relation to certain parts of the legal framework for the agreement. Consequently an attempt was made to ascertain first, when exclusion clauses will be drafted into agreements by businessmen and second, the circumstances in which they are relied upon during the grievance remedy procedures. For this purpose a survey was conducted amongst three groups of business operations in the south west and north west regions of England. Fifty-one firms co-operated in the survey, 31 being light or heavy mechanical or civil engineering firms, 12 being finance companies and eight being insurance companies or brokers. Fourteen of the firms who were prepared to answer questions about their practices had their own legal departments. There was quite a significant difference in the attitude of non-lawyer businessmen in firms with or without legal departments. Curiously lawyers, in the engineering industry particularly, appeared to be consulted at a much earlier stage in discussions on policy in firms without their own legal departments than they did in firms with legal departments.

The types of business dealt with by the firms consulted fell into two very distinct groups. First were those businesses who dealt mainly with other businessmen and whose contracts were thus geared to what one may term ''commercial'' operations, and secondly were those, mainly finance companies, who dealt with the general public and whose operations were in the consumer market. It is proposed to report the results of these two groups separately.

1. *Commercial agreements*

In so far as exclusion clauses were used at all, they tended to be of the following types. First they were used to prevent liability arising on the part of the supplier due to specified causes beyond his control, the most common being delay caused through strikes and the non-availability of materials. Secondly, they occasionally limited liability to a particular sum. Some firms thought these figures to be a genuine attempt to pre-estimate damages, although at least eight engineering firms expressed the view that the figures specified (usually varying amounts of the contract sum) were unlikely to bear much relation to the likely loss sustained.[18] All those firms felt that such terms were likely to avoid the necessity for litigation. There was, however, despite their favourable reception from the insurance companies, much opposition to their use from light engineering firms. Very common in contracts for the sale or supply of goods were various limitations as to time.[19] These took the form either of time limits on a party's right to go to arbitration or limits on the time within which claims must be made or notified. Exceptions designed to exclude liability in respect of express conditions or warranties of the contract were very rare and found in specially negotiated agreements rather than standard forms, although some firms, notably those with their own legal departments, confessed to having spent much time in drafting clauses that it was hoped would be successful in excluding the terms implied by the Sale of Goods Act 1893.[20] Various devices were adopted to make the clauses appear "reasonable," the most common being differential prices (putting a higher price on the goods supplied under a contract without the exclusion) or the offer of supply under some standard form terms which contained more onerous exclusions (such as those of the Federation of Associations of Specialists and Sub-contractors) as an alternative. None of the firms used contract documents that expressly excluded either the right to reject or rescind or the right to damages, although some firms did so by implication in that they *only* undertook to repair or replace defective goods.

By far the most common reason advanced for the incorporation of exclusion clauses into contracts was the desire to avoid court proceedings should something go wrong. This was the main justification advanced for clauses imposing arbitration, *Scott* v. *Avery* clauses,[21] time limit clauses and the "contingency" clauses. Distrust of the lawyer's ability to understand the businessman's problems was very marked.

Another reason frequently advanced was simply "because everyone else does it." This is not quite so mindless as it at first sounds. A very large number of contracts in the engineering industry are conducted by means of forms containing standard conditions of sale or purchase. The forms have the terms such as description of goods, price, delivery date, terms of payment, etc., on the front, whilst the terms providing for adjustment, contingencies and exclusions would be on the back. The buyer would frequently order in accordance with his conditions and the seller would acknowledge with his printed conditions. The exact correspondence between offer and acceptance was often difficult to determine and its significance clearly escaped many of the businessmen consulted. [22] Where lawyers had been involved in the drafting of these forms (which was by no means always the case) some attempt was often made to incorporate into the form certain terms and exclusions that were found in customers' forms, where these were not incompatable with the drafting firm's own business practices. Firms who did not secure the services of a lawyer in the drafting of their "back of order" conditions either drafted their own without legal assistance (25 per cent. of the sample of engineering firms) or used standard conditions such as those of the R.I.B.A. or the Institute of Civil Engineers (40 per cent. of the sample). Significantly all the insurance companies and finance houses received substantial legal assistance in drafting their terms. Comprehensive exclusions designed to provide protection should one's client find himself the victim of the other party's terms as a result of losing the "battle of the forms" were sometimes therefore adopted by insurance companies who had only agreed to provide cover if the contract were conducted by the client on *his* terms.

Those businesses dealing with complex pieces of machinery, such as engines, airframes, buses, etc., all tended to use meticulously drafted or specially negotiated written contracts. There was a preoccupation with the problems of possible patent infringement and several exclusion clauses attempted to deal with this difficulty. Section 12 of the Sale of Goods Act 1893 seemed to provide the greatest stumbling block in this regard and, in every case of a specially drafted contract for the sale of goods that the writer was shown, section 12(2) of the Act, rather than section 12(1) was incorporated.[23]

The final significant reason advanced for including some kind of exclusion clause in specially negotiated contracts was the desire to exclude or reduce liability for consequential loss. Since most of the specially negotiated contracts seemed to involve large, complex items such as bridges, buses, aircraft, etc., there was the risk that a defect could cause considerable consequential loss. In this area, rather than be his own insurer (which seemed to be the pattern with many businesses who dealt only on standard form or back of order terms) the manufacturer would take out extensive insurance cover. In many cases he would simply be passing on those risks the insurance company refused to cover at all, or would only cover with very high premium payments. One insurance company said that it insists on drafting the exclusions itself in any civil engineering contract which it is covering where the contract price exceeds one million pounds. Aside from these large, complex engineering items, however, most businesses appeared to insure against surprisingly few risks. Loss by fire and theft, loss in transit, damage by flood and sprinkler valves, loss through explosion and similar disasters causing destruction or damage and occasionally loss as a result of failure to meet delivery dates were covered. In all other respects the manufacturers were their own insurers. Surprisingly, no one was prepared to admit, however, that, aside from the problem of consequential loss, this was a factor that influenced whether a specially drafted contract should be commissioned from the legal department or the firm's solicitors, although it is hard to accept that it was not.

Both standard form and specially drafted contracts

contained numerous devices that were not actually exclusion clauses but clearly designed to achieve the same result. Contracts might provide that a representative of the other side could attend the pre-delivery inspections (and tests), and sometimes, notably with engines, the representative was asked to sign an acceptance note. Buyers sometimes provided that if a defect was not rectified within a particular time they might carry out the repair themselves at the seller's expense. Sometimes a buyer might impose the condition that the last instalment of the price would not be paid until the machine was operating satisfactorily in his own plant. Indeed the use of stipulations as to payment seemed to be trusted as more efficacious by the non-lawyers questioned than any liquidated damages clauses or exclusions. The insistence, for example, of cash with the order, or, on the buyer's part, no payment without satisfactory performance, seems like a clear attempt at self-regulation, obviating the need to seek the lawyer's services at all in grievance procedures.

2. *Consumer agreements*

In the consumer field all those companies questioned, both finance companies and insurance companies, used standard-form agreements. Contracts were never specially negotiated although occasionally forms of agreement seemed to be accepted from clients or customers with individual clauses struck out. Where this was done the firms concerned seemed to think that it made no difference to the terms of the agreement. One finance company said that applicants frequently strike out some (but rarely all) of the exclusion clauses in the standard form but that in the company's view this made no difference since by then the customer had been made aware of the terms upon which the company was prepared to contract. It is almost certain that the company's confidence in this matter was misplaced. Most proposal forms were sent in by the retail dealer or broker, already completed by the prospective client. After vetting the proposal, it would either be accepted or rejected by the company. The client was usually notified of acceptance by the statutorily required despatch of a second, executed copy of the agreement. The offer, then, came from the proposer, not the company, and if the proposal contains deleted clauses, and this is accepted by the company, then a binding contract on those terms would come into effect.

Most exclusions found in the standard form document related to exclusion of liability for misrepresentation (an attempt was frequently made to circumvent section 3 of the Misrepresentation Act 1967, by requiring agreement to a clause stating that the customer had not relied on any statements made to him[24]) and express conditions or warranties. Some attempts were still being made to exclude implied terms, notwithstanding the Supply of Goods (Implied Terms) Act 1973 and the Consumer Transactions (Restrictions on Statements) Order 1976.[25] The warranty of title was nearly always limited to such title as the company might have.[26] Hire-purchase forms usually contained a provision entitling the company to terminate the agreement for breach of any undertaking given by the hirer and there was also a provision excluding liability for personal injuries or consequential loss.

It was also common for hire-purchase agreements used by finance companies to contain clauses in which the hirer is expressed to acknowledge and agree a certain set of facts showing that the finance company as owner has complied with its liabilities (*e.g.* that the goods are in good condition and suitable for the purpose for which they are required) or that the requirements of the Hire-Purchase Act 1965[27] had been complied with, such as that the cash price was stated to the intending hirer before the agreement was entered into, that the clause excluding the statutory condition as to fitness was brought to the notice of the hirer and its effect made clear to him, and so on.[28] Finally, most agreements contained provisions permitting the company to rescind the agreement should there be any mistatement by the hirer and provisions requiring indemnity of the company by the hirer for any loss sustained consequent upon the agreement.

Most of the companies consulted were not particularly sanguine about the enforceability of the exclusion clauses in their agreements. Whilst they would, as a matter of policy, always be relied upon, their insertion seems to be largely a question of psychology. One representative of a finance company stated that the presence of exclusions is more likely to secure compliance with the agreement and far more likely to compel payment before the court hearing should the debt turn bad. All companies would enter bad debts on one of the two major credit reference agency lists and would pursue them rigorously, as a matter of policy, through the courts. The first stage would usually be a solicitor's letter followed by the repossession of the goods if possible and/or county court proceedings.

Most finance companies were prepared to admit, under pressure, that several of the retailers with whom they dealt did not always observe scrupulous standards of fair dealing. One legal advisor reported that the exclusion clauses in his company's agreements had a two-fold purpose. First, to protect the company against complaints about defects in the goods where those defects had been brought about by the hirer himself, and secondly to protect the company against unscrupulous retailers. The reducing chances of these clauses being upheld in litigation, as increasingly fierce attacks upon them are launched both by the legislature and the judiciary, has resulted in many finance companies turning away from the traditional hire-purchase agreement, sacrificing real security for the flexibility of personal loans or budget accounts. All the finance companies were, however, certain that these new devices were of a relatively short-lived efficacy, since, being mostly debtor-creditor-supplier agreements within the Consumer Credit Act 1974, s. 12, the lender will become liable for the retailer's breaches of contract and misrepresentations under section 75 of that Act even though the goods are purchased by the borrower from the retailer direct and not from the finance company. Most finance companies said that they would continue to use exclusion clauses in their agreements, simply because the "small print" clauses assisted in persuading the borrower to take his obligations seriously but no one doubted the impact that recent legislation had on the consumer credit field. Most of the companies reported turning to alternative forms of risk allocation and the insurance companies have reported a large increase in bad debt insurance from the smaller finance companies. Where repossession of the goods is difficult or impossible, and where the risk of defects can no longer be passed to the hirer, insurance is, perhaps, the only solution.

3. *Conclusions*

It seemed to all those enterprises questioned that detailed contract planning (though not necessarily specially negotiated contracts) had an important place in commercial practice, at least so far as the exclusion clauses were concerned. In those large businesses questioned that operated from more than one factory or office, for instance, the use of standard form contracts achieved a uniformity of dealing with all customers that could be decided on by head office. Certain issues could then be removed from future negotiation by branch managers and salesmen were unable to make concessions to the customer by altering back-of-order terms without first consulting the legal department or departmental head.

Also, businesses tended to feel that detailed planning and negotiation of contract terms was worth the time and cost in those cases where significant claims were likely to arise if something went wrong. The degree of injury in a case of default was especially significant and this factor, of course, cut both ways. For example, an airline is subject to claims from the survivors, and dependents of those killed in an air crash. Therefore, in buying planes from the airframe manufacturers the airlines insist on carefully defined and legally enforceable obligations. But an aircraft will usually be designed to operate with one and only one particular type of engine, so the aero-engine manufacturer has a virtual monopoly, at least so far as that particular design of aircraft is concerned. What started as a buyers' market, therefore, with the airline, finishes with a sellers' market with the engine. Hence the aero-engine manufacturer will impose rigorous exclusions against consequential loss which the airframe manufacturer cannot pass on to the airline. The intermediary risks must therefore be carried by insurance.

In the normal way, however, insurance was used rather less than expected. Commercial operators, who tend to be their own insurers,[29] use exclusion clauses far more to allocate risk, and thus, perhaps understandably, make use of specially drafted and negotiated exclusions to a greater extent than the consumer operator who tends to use exclusion clauses less to allocate risk than to attempt to convince the customer to take the contract seriously, or to settle out of court in a dispute. So far as legal sanctions or the threat of them are concerned, these are more readily resorted to by the consumer operator than the commercial. Although the consumer is less likely, generally speaking, to possess the means to meet judgment should he lose, as compared with the commercial customer, the finance company or the insurance company did not feel that frequent litigation was likely to do much harm to their businesses. Their trade did not seem to suffer according to how many law suits they were involved in. Managers and lawyers in the commercial market, on the other hand, took the totally opposite view. Good-will is very important in the engineering industry and a company that became known for resorting to the courts too frequently to settle disputes was likely to be avoided by potential customers. There was less fear of arbitration proceedings, for then the matter could be decided by someone with expertise in the particular industry. There was, however, a general reluctance to entrust the resolution of disputes to lawyers or the courts since generally speaking in commercial terms the costs were thought to outweigh the gains.

D. *Types of Exclusion Clause*

1. *Exemption from liability for breach*

These will be provisions in the contract that exclude or restrict the exercise of a right or remedy or any liability arising out of the breach of any obligation, express or implied, in the contract. So, a term in a civil engineering contract that the contractor's liability for failure to complete on the due date shall not exceed a specified figure, is such a clause. It would seem that such a clause is not an agreement for liquidated damages, since it is not a genuine pre-estimate of damage,[30] nor is it a penalty clause.[31] The clause does not, of course, destroy the contract and content of the initial promise, but simply qualifies the right to enforce the promise by imposing a limit on the quantum of damages recoverable.

Some clauses may go further and purport to exclude the right to damages or the right to reject altogether.[32] It could be argued that excluding the right to damages altogether is rather different in effect from simply limiting damages. By denying the remedy of damages the promisor is depriving his promise of any contractual content.[33] This is not the case with a clause denying the promisee the right to repudiate, since it leaves the remedy of damages intact.

Finally in this section are clauses that impose time limits, affect the question of how evidence is to be treated, or impose indemnity. Time limit clauses can be of two kinds. A clause may impose a time limit shorter than that fixed by the general law for the enforcement of a right or remedy or alternatively it may impose a time limit on action necessary before any right, remedy, duty or liability arises. An exclusion clause affecting evidence may be one altering the onus of proof of matters under the contract or providing that one matter is conclusive evidence of another. A case that provides a clause combining the effect of time limit clauses and clauses affecting evidentiary matters is that of *Buchanan* v. *Parnshaw*.[34] In that case a horse sold at auction was warranted to be six years old and sound. It was a term of the sale that, if the horse were unsound, it should be returned within two days, otherwise, it should be deemed sound. The failure to return within two days was therefore here made conclusive evidence of soundness. It is clear that any clause which requires the promisee to indemnify another as a consequence of the promisee having exercised a right or remedy under the contract is a provision restricting the exercise of a contractual right of remedy and is therefore an exclusion clause within the definition given at the start of this section.

2. *Arbitration Clauses*

An arbitration clause would seem to be only procedural in that a provision whereby the parties agree that any disputes should be submitted to arbitration does not exclude or limit rights or remedies, but simply provides a procedure under which the parties may settle their grievance. The courts have held that such a clause is not an exclusion clause proper[35] and the parties are free, such a clause notwithstanding, to pursue their claims in the courts,[36] subject to the right of the court to grant a stay of proceedings.[37] However, one type of arbitration clause can have substantive effect in that it can make the obligation to perform contingent upon the happening of an event. This clause is the so-called *Scott* v. *Avery*[38] clause, under which the parties agree that no action shall be brought upon the contract until the arbitrator's award has been made, or that the promisor's liability shall be to pay only such sum as an arbitrator shall award. However, notwithstanding the difference between these clauses and the more normal type of arbitration clause, the courts have still been reluctant to treat them as exclusion clauses[39] and the Law Commission, in its Second Report on Exemption Clauses, would not recommend that arbitration clauses be treated as other exclusion clauses.[40]

However, the Unfair Contract Terms Bill 1977[41] did contain one provision controlling arbitration clauses, but only where the party against whom the arbitration clause was being invoked dealt under the contract as a consumer (see Chap. 3). Clause 10(1) provided that such a clause could only be invoked when the consumer had given his written consent. This consent, however, was to be given *after* and not before differences between the parties had arisen, so the consent could not be given at the time the contract was made. The consumer himself could have implemented the arbitration procedure with no prior statutory requirement but where he did so he might then have had a clause providing for future differences to be referred to arbitration invoked against him without the need for him to give his written consent (cl. 10(1) (*b*)). These provisions did not affect arbitration clauses in contracts referred to in Schedule 1 to the Bill (cl. 10(2)(*b*)). The most important of these are insurance contracts, contracts creating or transferring interests in land, contracts dealing with patents, trade-marks, copyrights, etc., and intellectual property and contracts dealing with securities and the regulation of affairs between a company and its members. Aside from these provisions, agreements to submit present or future differences to arbitration were not treated as clauses excluding or restricting any liability (cl. 13(2)). The Act as it finally appeared does not treat *any* arbitration clause as an exemption (s. 13(2)).

3. *Liquidated damages clause*

A liquidated damages clause, unlike a clause that simply fixes maximum limit on the amount of damages recoverable, is a genuine attempt at a pre-estimate of damages.[42] Where, however, the contract stipulates for a named sum, not for the purpose of fixing in advance the loss which the parties consider is likely to flow from the breach but as a penalty, to secure performance of the contract, a claim on the penalty will succeed only to the extent of the loss actually suffered by the innocent party.[43] However, a valid liquidated damages clause may in practice limit the liability that would have been imposed on a party in breach of contract had there been no such provision. A provision for liquidated damages is not normally regarded as an exemption clause. In *Suisse Atlantique Société d'Armement Maritime S.A.* v. *N.V. Rotterdamische Kolen Centrale*[44] it was argued that a demurrage clause (a clause making a pre-estimate of damage caused to a shipowner by delay of the vessel in port after the date due for sailing) should be treated as an exemption clause, but Lord Upjohn distinguished between "clauses which are truly clauses of exception or limitation, that is to say clauses essentially inserted for the purpose only of protecting one contracting party from the legal consequences of other express terms of the contract or from terms which would otherwise be implied by law or from terms of the contract regarded as a whole" and clauses inserted for the benefit of both parties, such as agreed damages clauses.[45] A distinction was drawn in that case between a clause agreeing a figure of damages where no proof of loss was needed (a liquidated damages clause), and a clause imposing a limit where proof of loss at least up to the limit would be necessary (an exemption clause).[46]

4. *Excepted perils clauses and "promissory" warranties in contracts of insurance*

In the law of insurance, the use of the word "warranty"

should be clearly distinguished from its use in other branches of the law of contract. The usual use of the term is to denote a promise, the breach of which only entitles the party aggrieved to damages, leaving him still liable to perform his side of the bargain. A warranty in a policy of insurance, on the other hand, corresponds with a condition in any other contract,[47] and breach of it entitles the party aggrieved to repudiate his liability under the rest of the contract. Warranties relating to the future are sometimes described as "promissory" warranties.[48] This term is misleading, however, as most warranties are in a sense promissory.[49] In fact, in marine insurance "promissory" warranties are contrasted with warranties which merely define the risk insured against,[50] which can only relate to the future. These risk defining warranties, *e.g.* where in a policy of marine insurance a ship is "warranted free of capture" by an F.C. and S. clause,[51] are not warranties in the sense of conditions at all, they are simply excepted perils; breach of them does not entitle the insurer to repudiate all liability under the policy. So, if a vessel "warranted free of capture" is captured, the underwriters will not be responsible for that loss, but they will be liable for a subsequent loss by a peril of the sea, provided the capture was not the proximate cause of it.[52]

In general insurance law also, any representation that is warranted to be true is sometimes spoken of as being, for that reason, a "promissory" warranty.[53] Such "promissory" warranties or conditions precedent to the insurer's liability must be clearly distinguished from clauses in a contract describing or limiting the risk. It is customary for a policy, having defined the risk, to cut down its scope by means of exceptions or excepted perils. Such excepted perils are frequently printed among the conditions of the policy. They are not, however, conditions in the usual sense, but rather operate as limitations on the risk covered by the policy, exempting the insurers from liability for certain kinds of loss which would otherwise be covered by it.[54] So the occurrence of an excepted peril will not preclude the assured from recovery unless it is also the proximate cause of the loss. In the case of the breach of a promissory warranty the cause of the loss is immaterial, and any breach of the warranty entitles the insurers to repudiate even if it had nothing whatever to do with the loss.

Thus, in *Provincial Insurance* v. *Morgan*,[55] the assured stated that a lorry he insured was to be used to carry coal, and the cover was limited to transportation in connection with his business. He also warranted his answers to be true. He occasionally used the lorry to carry timber, but was involved in an accident when carrying coal only. It was held that the effect of his statement was only to limit the risk to the use of the lorry while carrying coal, and that he could therefore recover. His statement did not amount to a warranty that the lorry would only be used to carry coal. Similarly, in *Farr* v. *Motor Traders Mutual Insurance Society Ltd.*[56] a statement by the assured that a cab was only to be driven on one shift per 24 hours was held to be only a description of the risk, and was not construed as a warranty. In *De Maurier* (*Jewels*) v. *Bastion Insurance Co,*[57] Donaldson J. held that a warranty regarding locks and alarms fitted to vehicles was not of a promissory character; it delimited and was part of the description of the risk.

On the other hand, in *Palatine Insurance* v. *Gregory*[58] fire insurances on timber were made "subject to the fifty feet clear space clause attached." The clear space clause read: "Warranted by the assured that a clear space of fifty feet shall hereafter be maintained between the timber hereby insured and any sawmill." It was held that this clause amounted to a promissory warranty, and was not merely a limitation on the cover afforded. The problem is really one of construction as to whether the court finds the statement to be "promissory" or merely definitional of the risk covered.

5. *Additional clauses brought into control by the Unfair Contract Terms Act 1977*

The main aim of the Act is to bring into control by applying a test of reasonableness, clauses of exclusion and allied contractual terms, and to prohibit altogether certain types of exclusion, such as those excluding or restricting liability for death or personal injury resulting from negligence. The detailed provisions of the Act are discussed throughout this work. However, in addition to the types of clause already discussed, the Act attempts to impose controls on other contractual terms that might be thought to have a similar effect on risk to that of an exclusion clause.

First are indemnity clauses. By virtue of section 4(1) any person dealing as a consumer cannot be required under a term of the contract to indemnify another in respect of liability that may be incurred by that other for negligence or breach of contract except to the extent that the term is reasonable. The clause actually applies the reasonableness test on the clause *imposing* the liability to indemnify rather than on the terms of the indemnity itself, which may be contained in a different clause of the contract. It may be, therefore, that a court would have to rely on its general powers "to have regard to the circumstances" (in s. 11(1)) when deciding the question of reasonableness in order to review the actual terms of the indemnity. The provision applies whether the indemnity is given in favour of the other party to the contract or some third person, and is to operate whether the indemnity is in respect of a liability to the consumer himself or to someone else. It will also apply if the liability to be indemnified is vicarious.

The Act also contains provisions regulating exclusions in guarantees and explains, in section 13(1), the meaning of the phrase "exclude or restrict liability," which is used throughout the Act. These matters are discussed later in Chapter 4. However, section 13(1) also clarifies one other matter. The

Act, as we shall see, makes void or ineffective terms which exclude or restrict liability in respect of certain implied obligations (*e.g.* in consumer contracts for work and materials, see Chap. 3). A common form of exemption clause is one which purports to exclude "all conditions and warranties, express or implied." This sub-section therefore also provides that terms which exclude or restrict the conditions or warranties themselves (rather than liability for their breach) are within those controls in the Act which are expressed to apply to exclusion or restriction of liability. Similarly there are controls over clauses restricting or excluding liability for negligence. Section 13(1) provides that terms or notices which exclude or restrict the duty of care itself, or the contractual obligation to take care, are within the controls in the Act expressed to apply to exclusions and limitations. This provision is not, however, made to apply to section 4 of the Act. Hence the problem, previously adverted to, of controlling indemnities where the obligation to indemnify, and the terms on which indemnity must be made, are split up into different terms of the contract.

Notes

1 See Sales, "Standard Form Contracts" (1953) 16 M.L.R. 318; Isaacs, "The Standardization of Contracts," 27 Yale L.J.34 (1917); Prausnitz, "Standardization of Commercial Contracts in English and Continental Law," *passim*; Llewellyn, "What Price Contract — An Essay in Perspective," 40 Yale L.J. 704 (1931); Kessler, "Contracts of Adhesion," 43 Colum. L. Rev. 629 (1943); Wilson, "Contracts of Adhesion and the Freedom of Contract," (1965) 14 I.C. L.Q. 172; Patterson, "The Interpretation and Construction of Contracts," 64 Colum. L. Rev. 833, 857 (1964); Berlioz, *Le Contrat D'Adhesion* (2nd ed.), *passim*.

2 The term "standard-form contract" is not a term of art, and has no technical meaning. Legislation in Israel has, however, attempted a statutory definition: "a contract ... all or any of whose terms have been fixed in

advance by, or on behalf of, the person supplying the commodity or service ... with the object of constituting conditions of many contracts between him and persons undefined as to their number or identity ... " Standard Contracts Law 5724, 1964, S.1.

3   See, *e.g. Trade and Transport Inc.* v. *Iino Kaiun Kaisha* [1973] 1 W.L.R. 210.

4   See, *e.g.* Brazier, (1976) 40 Conv. (N.S.) 179.

5   Eörsi, "The Validating of Clauses Excluding or Limiting Liability," 23 Am.J.Comp. L. 215, (1975); see also Berlioz, *Le Contrat D'Adhesion* (2nd ed.), Chap. 1.

6   See Devlin, "The Relation Between Commercial Law and Commercial Practice" (1951) 14 M.L.R. 249.

7   Report on the U.S.A. law on exemption clauses delivered to the 1Xth International Congress of Comparative Law, Teheran, 1974, by John G. Flemming, p. 106.

8   [1977] 3 W.L.R. 90, at pp. 94-95.

9   [1974] 1 W.L.R. 1308 at p. 1316.

10   K. Galbraith, *American Capitalism, The Countervailing Power,* Chap. 9.

11   See Pigou, *Economics of Welfare* (4th ed.), *passim;* Coase, 111 J. of Law & Econ. 1 (1960); Stigler, *The Theory of Price* (3rd ed.), 113 *et seq.*; Calabresi, 38 Harv. L.Rev.713 (1965); Nutter, 11 J. of Law & Econ. 503 (1968); Cheung, "Transaction Cost, Risk Aversion and the Choice of Contractual Arrangements," 12 J. of Law & Econ. 23 (1969). See also Coase, "The Nature of the Firm," N.S.4 Economica 386 (1937).

12   Pigou, *Economics of Welfare* (4th ed.), *passim.*

13   See "The Technique Element in Law," 59 Calif. L. Rev. 733 (1971).

14   [1967] 2 Lloyd's Rep. 61.

15   At p. 67.

16   Macaulay, "Non-Contractual Relations in Business," 28 Am. Sociological Rev. 45 (1963); see also Kawashima, "Dispute Resolution in Contemporary Japan," in, *Law in Japan: The Legal Order of a Changing Society,* pp. 41-52, (ed. Taylor von Mehred).

17   (1975) 2 Br. J. Law and Society 45.

18   See Coote, *Exception Clauses,* pp. 153-154.

19   *Ibid.* pp. 154-156.

20   See *post,* Chap. 3.

21   (1856) L.J. Ex.308. This is a clause whereby the parties agree that the promisor's only liability shall be to pay whatever sum an arbitrator shall award.

22   See Hoggett, "Changing a Bargain By Confirming It" (1970) 33 M.L.R. 518.

23   See *post,* p. 69.

24 See *post*, p. 58.
25 See *post*, p. 67.
26 See *post*, p. 73, n. 50.
27 At the time of the survey, no part of the Consumer Credit Act 1974 that affected regulated consumer agreements under that Act was in force.
28 *Cf. Lowe* v. *Lombank Ltd.* [1960] 1 A11 E.R.611.
29 Except that most sellers with an export market tended to use the Export Credit Guarantee Scheme, which covers 90 per cent. of the price.
30 *Cf. Cellulose Acetate Silk Co.* v. *Widnes Foundry* [1933] A.C.20.
31 *Cellulose Acetate Silk Co.* v. *Widnes Foundry, ante; cf. Dunlop Pneumatic Tyre Co. Ltd.* v. *New Garage and Motor Co. Ltd.* [1915] A.C.79.
32 See Montrose (1937) 15 Can. B. Rev. 760 at p. 781.
33 See Coote, *Exception Clauses,* pp. 152-153.
34 (1788) 2 Term Rep. 745.
35 *Atlantic Shipping Co.* v. *Dreyfus* [1922] 2 A.C. 250, *per* Viscount Dunedin at p. 258; *Woolf* v. *Collis* [1948] 1 K.B. 11; *cf. Hamlyn* v. *Talisker Distillery* [1894] A.C.202.
36 *Doleman & Sons* v. *Ossett Corporation* [1912] 3 K.B. 257.
37 Arbitration Act 1950, s.4(1); Arbitration Act 1975, s.1.
38 (1856) L.J. Ex. 308.
39 *Woolf* v. *Collis* [1948] 1 K.B. 11, *per* Asquith L.J. at p. 17.
40 Law Commission, *Second Report on Exemption Clauses,* Law Com. No. 69, para. 163.
41 *Post*, pp. 56-64.
42 *Dunlop Pneumatic Tyre Co. Ltd.* v. *New Garage & Motor Co. Ltd.* [1915] A.C.79.
43 *Wall* v. *Rederiaktiebolaget Luggude* [1915] 3 K.B. 66; *Watts, Watts & Co. Ltd.* v. *Mitsui & Co. Ltd.* [1917] A.C.227.
44 [1967] 1 A.C. 361.
45 *Ibid.* at p. 420.
46 *Ibid. per* Viscount Dilhorne at p. 395; *per* Lord Upjohn at pp. 420-421; *per* Lord Wilberforce at p. 436.
47 *E.g.* that the assured will not proceed abroad, or that he will fit a mortise lock within a given time to his front door. Until breach the insurers are bound; a breach, even after the contract is complete, relieves the insurers from subsequent liability.
48 See, *e.g.* Marine Insurance Act 1906, s.33(1).
49 *Provincial Insurance* v. *Morgan* [1933] A.C. 240, *per* Lord Wright at p. 254.
50 *Re Morgan & another and Provincial Insurance Co. Ltd.* [1932] 2 K.B. 70, *per* Scrutton L.J. at p. 80.
51 Free of capture and seizure. The letters are used in policies of marine

insurance to indicate that the underwriter is not to be liable for capture or seizure of either the ship or the cargo resulting from the action of enemies, or of pirates, or of the owner's own government or of a foreign government.

52 *Anderson* v. *Marten* [1908] A.C.334.

53 *Provincial Insurance* v. *Morgan* [1933] A.C.240, *per* Lord Wright at p. 254; *cf. Hearts of Oak* v. *Law Union* [1936] 2 A11 E.R. 619, *per* Goddard J. at p. 623.

54 *Re Hooley Hill Rubber and Royal Insurance Co. Ltd.* [1920] 1 K.B. 257, *per* Duke L.J. at p. 274; *Lake* v. *Simmons* [1927] A.C.487, *per* Viscount Sumner at p. 507.

55 [1933] A.C. 240.

56 [1920] 3 K.B. 669.

57 [1967] 2 Lloyd's Rep. 550.

58 [1926] A.C. 90.

Chapter 2

THE CONTRACTUAL FORCE OF EXCLUSION

A. *Incorporation into Contracts*

An exclusion clause will only operate to limit or modify contractual rights or remedies when it has been incorporated into the contract upon which it purports to have effect. This, on the face of it rather obvious, statement is no more than a particular example of the general proposition that not all the words which the parties said or wrote during their negotiations will become part of the contract. If the contract is wholly oral, its contents are a matter of fact to be established by evidence proving what the parties said and intended. If the contract is wholly written then there will rarely be any dispute of fact as to what was agreed, but instead a dispute as to what the words used actually mean, which is a matter of interpretation for the judge.[1] However, where the contract is wholly in writing, extrinsic evidence is generally inadmissable when it would, if accepted, have the effect of adding to, varying or contradicting the terms of a document constituting a valid and effective contract. In *Bank of Australia* v. *Palmer*[2] Lord Morris said[3]: "Parol testimony cannot be received to contradict, vary, add to or subtract from the terms of a written contract, or the terms in which the parties have deliberately agreed to record any part of their contract."[4]

Were this to be an unshakeable principle of contractual construction there would be no occasion when an exclusion clause, not found in the original written contract, would bind the parties. This is not, however, the case.[5] Evidence may be admitted to prove a custom or trade usage, notwithstanding the absence of any mention of such matters in the written document. Indeed, the practical effect of the "parol evidence rule" can be completely negatived by the court finding that the document only contains part of the terms, *i.e.* the contract was made partly in writing and partly by word of mouth or by conduct. Whilst the presence of writing raises a presumption that the writing contains the whole contract,[6] this presumption may be rebutted by evidence that the parties did not intend the writing to be exclusive.[7] In the context of exemption clauses, therefore, it may be possible for the party seeking to rely on the clause to argue that, notwithstanding its apparent absence from the contractual document in question, that document does not represent the entire contract between the parties and a clause of exclusion should still apply[8] because, for instance, the parties intended it to be implied into their agreement from a previous course of dealing.

The problems created by attempts to incorporate exclusion clauses from previous dealings between the parties into contracts, whether those contracts be written or oral, are not new[9] although there is little doubt that the attitude of the judiciary towards them has changed radically as the "consumer interest" has displaced the "commercial interest" as the area of primary intervention.[10] The courts initially took the view that businessmen who were used to dealing with each other over a long period on virtually identical terms on each occasion, may not necessarily read all the contract documents every time, but simply assume them to be in conformity with the previous course of dealing.[11] That being so, incorporation of an exclusion clause into the instant contract could be inferred from a previous course of dealing between the parties. For instance, in *J. Spurling Ltd.* v. *Bradshaw*[12] the defendant delivered eight barrels of orange juice to the plaintiff warehousemen, with whom he had frequently dealt in the past. Some days later the defendant received a "landing account" acknowledging receipt of the barrels and referring on its face to a set of "contract conditions" printed on the back. These conditions contained a clause purporting to exempt the plaintiffs from liability for loss or damage "occasioned by the negligence, wrongful act or default" of themselves, their servants or agents. When the defendant eventually collected the barrels some were empty, some contained dirty water and the rest were leaking badly. The defendant failed to pay the storage charges and the plaintiffs sued him. The defendant counterclaimed for damages alleging that the plaintiffs either were in breach of an implied term of the contract of bailment to take reasonable care of the barrels or were guilty of negligence in the storage. The plaintiffs pleaded the exemption clause but the defendant argued that since he had only received the "landing account" after conclusion of the contract, the exclusion clauses contained therein should not affect him. However, the defendant did give evidence to the effect that he had received many landing accounts from the plaintiffs in the past in respect of other goods but that he had never read them. As a result of this previous course of business dealing between the parties the defendant was held to be bound by the clause which had thus become incorporated into the instant contract.

Despite the view of Lord Devlin that cases in which terms will be implied into agreements by usage or by course of dealing between the parties will be of increasing rarity in modern commercial practice,[13] it still appears to be relatively easy to show that terms are included in a contract by a course of dealing. In *British Crane Hire Corporation* v. *Ipswich Plant Hire*[14] the plaintiffs and the defendants were both engaged in the business of hiring out earth-moving equipment. The defendants were also involved in draining some marshy ground and urgently required a crane. They agreed to hire a crane from the plaintiffs. The terms of payment were agreed but no mention was made of the plaintiffs' conditions of hire. The plaintiffs sent the defendants a copy of such conditions which provided, *inter alia*, that the hirer would be responsible for all expenses arising out of the crane's use. Before the defendants signed the form containing the conditions, the crane sank into the marsh through no fault of the defendants and the plaintiffs claimed the cost of recovering the crane. The Court of Appeal held that since the bargaining power of the defendants was equal to that of the plaintiffs, and the defendants knew that printed conditions in similar terms to those of the plaintiffs were in common use in the business, the plaintiffs were entitled to conclude that the defendants were accepting the crane on the terms of their conditions. The conditions had therefore been incorporated into the contract on the basis of the common understanding of the parties and accordingly the plaintiffs' claim succeeded.

It would appear to follow from this that where the bargaining power of the parties is not equal, as it rarely is in the consumer context,[15] implication of terms by reference to a previous course of dealing is far more difficult. Whilst it does sometimes happen that the doctrine enunciated in *J. Spurling Ltd.* v. *Bradshaw*[16] is applied in consumer cases,[17] it is comparatively rare. For example, in *Hollier* v. *Rambler Motors* (*A.M.C.*) *Ltd.*[18] the plaintiff telephoned the defendants' garage and asked if they would repair his car. The defendants' manager said that they would if the plaintiff had it towed to the garage. While in the garage the car was damaged by a fire which started as a result of the garage's negligence. On three or four occasions in the previous five years the plaintiff had had repairs carried out at the garage and on each of those occasions had signed a form which stated that "The Company is not responsible for damage caused by fire to customer's cars on the premises." In an action by the plaintiff claiming damages for negligence the defendants contended that, although the plaintiff had not signed the form on this occasion, the exemption clause had been incorporated in the oral contract between them by a course of dealing, and that its effect was to exclude liability for negligently causing a fire whilst the car was in their care. The Court of Appeal held *inter alia* that the defendants were liable to the plaintiff because three or four transactions in the course of five years were not sufficient to establish a course of dealing and so the clause was not incorporated into the oral contract. Commenting on that decision, Lord Denning M.R. observed[19]: "That was a case of a private individual who had had his car repaired by the defendants and had signed forms with conditions on three or four occasions. The plaintiff there was not of equal bargaining power with the garage company which repaired the car. The conditions were not incorporated." The implication is clear. Had the parties both been commercial men, contracting on equal terms, the result might well have been different.

However, of equal significance in the *Hollier* case, and other cases in which a previous pattern of business is relied upon to incorporate an exclusion clause into a contract, is the problem of what constitutes a previous course of dealing between the parties. Some degree of regularity of conduct is required but the precise amount is subject to doubt. In *Spurling Ltd.* v. *Bradshaw,*[20] for example, it was merely stated that the defendant "had received many landing accounts before."[21] In *Henry Kendall and Sons* v. *William Lillico and Sons*[22] a contract of sale was made orally by one Golden on the Bury St. Edmunds Corn Exchange for the sale of poultry feeding stuffs to the Suffolk Agricultural Poultry Producers Association Ltd. by Grimsdale and Sons Ltd. On the following day Grimsdale sent a confirmation note to the Association which contained on its back conditions of sale. As the parties had on many previous occasions made contracts in just such a way, both the Court of Appeal and the

House of Lords held that the conditions of sale formed part of the contract since both parties were deemed to have contracted on that basis. The frequency of previous dealing here was three or four agreements a month in the previous three years involving the use of such confirmation notes. In *British Crane Hire Corp.* v. *Ipswich Plant Hire Ltd.*[23] there were only two transactions many months before, although there was also trade usage to take account of. In *Hollier* v. *Rambler Motors (A.M.C.) Ltd.*,[24] on the other hand, there were three or four transactions over a period of five years yet this was not sufficient to show a course of dealing, although, as has already been noted, this may, partially at least, depend upon the fact that the latter case involved a "consumer" as opposed to a "commercial" transaction.

It would seem, therefore, that the previous course of dealing must at least be consistent and regular, although there is no evidence that the courts require proof that the parties have deemed themselves to be bound by the particular clause in question. Also, provided that there is sufficient regularity, the terms of the disputed document will be implied into the contract even though the terms of the document have not remained constant, as long as the recipient has reasonable notice that there are terms. Thus, in *Spurling Ltd.* v. *Bradshaw*[25] Morris L.J. observed[26]: "It is true ... that because the evidence of the plaintiff was not heard, there is no positive evidence that the conditions on previous landing accounts were the same as the conditions in the present case. But it is clearly established[27] that Mr. Bradshaw knew that there were conditions."[27]

This last observation is perhaps dependent upon the view that it is simply constructive knowledge of the term to be implied, rather than actual knowledge, that is material. This is contrary to the opinion expressed by Lord Devlin in the House of Lords in *McCutcheon* v. *David MacBrayne Ltd.*[28] In that case the appellant asked a Mr. McSporran to arrange for the shipment of his, the appellant's, car to the Scottish mainland on one of the respondents' steamers. McSporran made an oral contract on the appellant's behalf at the respondents' office, for shipment and was given a receipted invoice, which he did not read. The respondents' conditions of carriage excluded liability for their own negligence and these conditions were exhibited in the respondents' office and on board their vessels. The receipted invoice also contained a statement that the goods were carried subject to the conditions set out in the respondents' notices. It was the respondents' usual practice to ask a consignor to sign a risk note, by which the consignor agreed to be bound by the respondents' conditions, which were printed on it. In the circumstances under dispute a risk note was made out before delivery of the car but, owing to an oversight, McSporran was not asked to and did not sign it. However, McSporran had shipped goods in a similar manner before and he had sometimes signed risk notes but he had never read them nor the conditions displayed in the office or on board. The appellant also had consigned goods through the respondents before, but he had never read the conditions or any risk notes either, although he knew that conditions of some kind existed. On the voyage the ship sank owing to the respondents' negligent navigation, and the car was lost. In an action for damages the respondents relied on the exclusions clause which, they argued, was imported into the contract by reason of the previous dealings between the parties.

The House of Lords gave judgment for the appellant. Neither he nor McSporran had read the conditions and there was, therefore, only an oral contract. The respondents had not discharged the burden of showing knowledge on the part of the appellant of the terms of the conditions and accordingly liability on the part of the respondents for negligence was not excluded. Lord Devlin[29] expressed the view that previous dealings are relevant only if they prove **actual** knowledge of the terms, rather than constructive knowledge of them, and also prove assent to them by the other party. This view almost certainly goes too far and has been subsequently criticised[30] in that it fails to have regard to the fact that in English law the test of contractual formation is objective. In the words of Diplock L.J.[31]:

"The task of ascertaining what the parties to a contract of any kind have agreed shall be their legal rights and liabilities to one another as a result of the contract ... is accomplished not by determining what each party actually thought those rights and liabilities should be, but by what each party by his words and conduct reasonably led the other party to believe were the acts which he was undertaking a legal obligation to perform."

In *McCutcheon* v. *David MacBrayne Ltd.*[32] the usual procedure of signing a written note of the terms was not adopted. Lord Pearce stated[33] that the ordinary course of business could not be of help to the carrier, since the transaction did not follow the ordinary course, no written contract having been supplied. This does seem a more satisfactory explanation of the result than Lord Devlin's reliance on actual as against constructive knowledge.[34]

B. *The Effect of Signature*

Where a contractual document is signed by a party, the fact of agreement is proved by his signature and, in the absence of fraud or misrepresentation, or the availability of the plea of *non est factum,*[35] it is wholly immaterial that he has not read the contract and does not know its contents or even that he cannot speak or read English. He will therefore be unable to argue that he has no notice of an exclusion clause contained in a contractual document to which he has put his signature.[36] Thus, in *L'Estrange* v. *Graucob*[37] the plaintiff agreed to purchase from the defendants a cigarette vending machine. The agreement provided for payment by instalments and it contained a clause excluding liability for breaches of warranty or condition. The plaintiff signed the agreement without readings its terms. The machine was faulty and the plaintiff purported to terminate for breach of condition. It was held that she could not do so since the exemption clause had effectively excluded all liability on the part of the seller. Scrutton L.J. said[38]:

"In cases in which the contract is contained in a railway ticket or other unsigned document, it is necessary to prove that an alleged party was aware, or ought to have been aware, of its terms and conditions. These cases have no application when the document has been signed. When a document containing contractual terms is signed, then, in the absence of fraud, or, I will add, misrepresentation, the party signing it is bound, and it is wholly immaterial whether he has read the document or not."

In some cases, however, the absolute effect of the signature will not be enforced. So, where an employee of a dry cleaning firm misrepresented to the customer the true purpose of the receipt signed by the customer, the Court of Appeal held that the defendant company were precluded from enjoying the full force of their exemption clause contained therein.[39] Statute has also had some impact in this area. As is discussed in the next chapter certain statutory provisions have rendered exclusion clauses either prima facie void,[40] or of no effect if it can be shown to be unfair to permit reliance on them.[41] These statutory provisions will operate on an exclusion clause contained in a contractual document, notwithstanding its signature.

C. *Written Clauses of Exclusion*

It will rarely be the case that an exclusion clause will be oral.

In theory there is nothing against this but in practice the evidentiary problems make it unlikely. Thus, exclusion or exemption clauses will normally be written, either within the contract itself, or upon notices, tickets, receipts or other documents which the party seeking to rely on them hopes to incorporate into the transaction. In those cases in which the contract is partly oral and partly written the party seeking to rely on the exclusion clause will have to show that he has incorporated it into the bargain between the parties. As we have seen, this may be done by reference to a previous course of dealing between the parties, or by signature of the written part of the transaction. In the absence of either of these possibilities the exclusion clause will only be treated as part of the agreement if it has been brought to the notice of the party affected by it.[42]

There has been a very great deal of litigation on the problem of what constitutes sufficient notice of a written exemption clause for it to be regarded as part of the agreement. The first point of significance here is the timing of the notice in that for a term to become a binding part of the contract it must be brought to the notice of the party affected by it, and he must expressly or impliedly assent to it, before or at the time that the contract is made. The classic illustration of this principle is to be found in *Olley* v. *Marlborough Court Ltd.*[43] where the plaintiff and her husband booked in and paid for in advance a week's board and residence in the defendants' hotel. They then went up to their room where a notice was exhibited which contained the clause: "The proprietors will not hold themselves responsible for articles lost or stolen unless handed to the manageress for safe custody." Owing to the negligence of the hotel staff in allowing a third party access to the room key, the wife's furs were stolen. The plaintiff sued and the defendants attempted to rely on the exclusion clause, arguing that it had been incorporated into the contract by the notice in the room. The Court of Appeal held that the contract was made at the reception desk when the defendants agreed to accept the week's booking from the plaintiff. The notice could not, therefore, form part of the contract since the plaintiff could not have seen it until after the contract was made and the defendants were thus liable for the loss.

This problem can be raised in a particularly striking form when the contract is concluded through the medium of an automatic machine. Insofar as notice of any exclusion clause must be given before or at the time of concluding the agreement, the precise moment when the offer is accepted, and indeed the question of who makes the offer and who the acceptance, is of especial significance where the contract is concluded through the medium of a machine which accepts money or tokens. In *Thornton* v. *Shoe Lane Parking Ltd.* [44] the plaintiff drove his car into a car park which had an automatic barrier. He had never been there before. A notice outside gave the charges and stated that all cars were "parked at owner's risk." A traffic light at the entrance showed red and a machine produced a ticket when the car stopped beside it. The plaintiff took the ticket and, the light having turned green, drove into the garage and parked his car. On returning to collect it there was an accident in which he was injured. In his action against the garage for damages the garage contended, *inter alia*, that the ticket incorporated a condition exempting them from liability. The ticket stated the car's time of arrival and that it was to be presented when the car was claimed. In the bottom left-hand corner in small print it was said to be "issued subject to conditions ... displayed on the premises." On a pillar opposite the ticket machine were displayed eight lengthy conditions, one of which stated that the garage owners were not responsible for injury to a customer.[45] The Court of Appeal held that the plaintiff was not bound by the conditions printed on the ticket; the contract was concluded when the car was driven to the entrance of the garage, causing the ticket to be issued, and the plaintiff could not be bound by conditions brought to his attention after this. Lord Denning M.R. characterised the problem as being one of offer and acceptance thus[46]:

"The customer pays his money and gets a ticket. He cannot refuse it. He cannot get his money back. He may protest to the machine, even swear at it. But it will remain unmoved. He is committed beyond recall. He was committed at the very moment when he put his money into the machine. The contract was concluded at that time. It can be translated into offer and acceptance in this way: the offer is made when the proprietor of the machine holds it out as being ready to receive the money. The acceptance takes place when the customer puts his money into the slot. The terms of the offer are contained in the notice placed on or near the machine, stating what is offered for the money. The customer is bound by these terms as long as they are sufficiently brought to his notice beforehand, but not otherwise. He is not bound by the terms printed on the ticket if they differ from the notice, because the ticket comes too late. The contract has already been made."[47]

This case, whilst specifically involving an automatic machine, raises in a general sense a further point concerning the adequacy of the notice that must be given by a party seeking to rely on an exclusion clause. The Court of Appeal held that in order to show that the plaintiff was bound by the conditions exempting the garage from liability, it was necessary to show either that he knew of it or that the garage proprietor had done what was reasonably necessary to draw it to his attention. For this purpose, where the clause was unusual in the particular type of contract in which it was found, or was exceptionally wide or destructive of the plaintiff's rights, it was insufficient to show simply that the plaintiff had been given notice that the ticket was issued subject to conditions.

The defendant must also establish that adequate steps had been taken to draw the plaintiff's attention in the most explicit way to the particular clause relied on. This had not been done and so the plaintiff's action succeeded on this ground.

Such a line of argument concerning the reasonableness of the notice that must be given in such cases has an old and respected pedigree, stemming from the judgment of Mellish L.J. delivered in 1877 in *Parker* v. *South Eastern Railway*.[48] Lord Hodson, commenting on the judgment of Mellish L.J., has said that the correct questions to ask in a ticket case were[49]:

(1)   Did the person receiving the ticket know that there was printing on it? If not, he is not bound.

(2)   Did he know that the ticket contained or referred to conditions? If he did, then he will be bound.

(3)   Did the party seeking to rely on the clause do what was reasonable in the way of notifying prospective contracting parties of the existence of conditions and where their terms might be considered? If he did then, notwithstanding the other party's lack of knowledge as under (1) above, then the clause will be part of the contract. If he did not then, unless (2) above applies, the conditions will not be a part of the contract.

It is the third of these questions that relates to the reasonableness of the notice given that causes the most difficulty. This is a question of fact[50] requiring the court to look at all the circumstances and the particular and respective positions of the parties.[51] A very high onus is placed on the party wishing to incorporate a clause that is unusual in that class of contract, or which imposes severe limitations on the other party's rights under the agreement.[52] In the words of Denning L.J.: "Some clauses which I have seen would need to be printed in red ink on the face of the document with a red hand pointing to it before the notice could be held to be sufficient."[53]

It is also usual to state on the face of the ticket that there are conditions printed on the back. If this is not done,[54] or the words are illegible[55] or buried in advertising material [56] the notification will be defective. Strictly the issue is one of fact, so there is no rule as to any of these matters,[57] but anyone seeking to rely on a clause who fails to have regard to them is virtually certain to fail.

The test of reasonableness, however, is an objective one, so that the fact that the plaintiff is under some disability, for instance, that he is blind or illiterate[58] or cannot speak English[59] is irrelevant, provided that the notice is reasonably sufficient for a person normally entering into such a transaction who is not under the disability. So, in *Thompson* v. *London, Midland and Scottish Railway Co.*[60] the plaintiff, who was illiterate, asked her niece to purchase for her a railway excursion ticket on the face of which were the words: "For conditions see back." The words on the back of the ticket stated that the ticket was issued subject to the conditions set out in the company's timetables, which could be obtained at a charge of 6d. The conditions in the timetable exempted the company from liability in respect of injury, however caused. The plaintiff suffered injuries on the trip as a result of the company's negligence and, in proceedings against the company for damages, was met by the exemption clause. The Court of Appeal held that the defendant company had taken reasonable steps to bring the conditions to the notice of ordinary travellers and the particular illiteracy of the plaintiff was irrelevant. Hence the defendants were not liable.

It is by no means clear, however, that the same result would pertain where the person seeking to rely on the clause knows of the particular disability of the other party. For instance, in *Richardson, Spence and Co.* v. *Rowntree*[61] the plaintiff contracted with the defendants for steerage passage from

Philadelphia to Liverpool. The ticket contained a number of printed terms including one limiting the defendants' liability to $100. The ticket was handed to the plaintiff folded up, and the conditions were partly obliterated by a stamp mark. She sustained injuries during the voyage and sued the defendants. The jury found that, although the plaintiff was aware that there was writing on the ticket, she did not know that the writing contained conditions. Accordingly, the jury found that the defendants had not given reasonably sufficient notice and the House of Lords refused to interfere with this finding. The main distinction between this and *Thompson's* case seems to be the view expressed by the House of Lords that the steerage passengers were likely to belong to a class of persons who could not be expected to read clauses in small print. It could be argued from this that if the party affected by the clause is known, for whatever reason, to be unable to read it, then far greater diligence is required of the party seeking to rely on the clause to bring it to the other's attention before the notice will be held to be reasonable.

One factor that will clearly affect the reasonableness of the notice is the kind of document in which the exclusion clause is contained. In *Parker* v. *South-Eastern Railway Co.,*[62] Mellish L.J. said[63]:

"I think there may be cases in which a paper containing writing is delivered by one party to another in the course of a business transaction, where it would be quite reasonable that the party receiving it should assume that the writing contained in it no condition, and should put it in his pocket unread. For instance, if a person driving through a turnpike-gate received a ticket upon paying the toll, he might reasonably assume that the object of the ticket was that by producing it he might be free from paying toll at some other turnpike-gate, and might put it in his pocket unread."

This principle was relied upon by the Court of Appeal in the case of *Chapleton* v. *Barry U.D.C.*[64] In this case the plaintiff hired one of the defendants' deck-chairs for the beach, paying 2d. and receiving a ticket in return from the attendant. After making a careful reconnaissance of appropriate sites, he set up the chair on the beach, and sat on it and fell through the canvas. He suffered personal injuries as a result and when he sued the defendants for damages, they set up the exemption clause printed on the back of the ticket as a defence. The plaintiff admitted that he had glanced at the ticket, but had not realised that it contained conditions. The Court took the view that such a ticket was not of a type that one would normally regard as a contractual document, and thus one would not reasonably expect it to contain contractual conditions. So, the defendants were not protected by the exemption clause since the ticket was simply a voucher or receipt. It did not purport to set out the conditions of hire but merely to show for how long the chair had been hired and that the hire charge had been paid.

Simply calling a document "a receipt" does not, however, automatically prevent it from being treated as "a contractual document."[65] It may be intended by the parties to have this effect or be delivered to the party to be affected by the conditions in such circumstances as to give him reasonable notice of them.[66] Whether a document is or is not a "contractual" document, *i.e.* one that could reasonably be expected to contain contractual terms, is a question of fact that may change with commercial[67] or consumer[68] practices.

Notes

1   *Bentsen* v. *Taylor, Sons & Co.* (*No. 2*) [1893] 2 Q.B. 274; *Bahamas International Trust Co. Ltd.* v. *Threadgold* [1974] 1 W.L.R. 1514.

2 [1897] A.C. 540.

3 At p. 545.

4 See also *Goss* v. *Lord Nugent* (1833) 5 B. & Ad. 58; *Jacobs* v. *Batavia and General Plantations Trust* [1924] 1 Ch.287, *per* P. O. Lawrence J. at p. 295; Wigmore, 4 Colum. L.Rev. 33-7 (1904); Wedderburn [1959] C.L.J.58.

5 *Roe* v. *Naylor* (1918) 87 L.J.K.B. 958; *Henry Kendall & Sons* v. *William Lillico & Sons* [1969] 2 A.C.31; Hoggett (1970) 33 M.L.R. 518.

6 *Gillespie Bros.* v. *Cheney, Eggar & Co.* [1896] 2 Q.B. 59, *per* Lord Russell of Killowen C.J. at p. 62; Wedderburn [1959] C.L.J.58; see also *Hutton* v. *Watling* [1948] Ch. 398.

7 *Walker Property Investments (Brighton) Ltd.* v. *Walker* (1947) 177 L.T.204; *Couchman* v. *Hill* [1947] K.B.554; *Ardennes (Cargo Owners)* v. *Ardennes (Owners)* [1951] 1 K.B.55.

8 *Roe* v. *Naylor* (1918) 87 L.J.K.B. 958.

9 *Crooks* v. *Allan* (1879) 5 Q.B.D. 38.

10 This has also been the experience in the U.S.A.; see 25 Notre Dame L.R.64.

11 Hoggett, "Changing a Bargain by Confirming It" (1970) 33 M.L.R. 518.

12 [1956] 1 W.L.R. 461.

13 Devlin, *Samples of Law Making* (1962), pp. 31-32.

14 [1975] Q.B.303.

15 Waddams, *Products Liability* (1974); Law Commission, *Exemption Clauses in Contracts, First Report,* Law Com. No. 24 (1969); Law Commission, *Exemption Clauses in Contracts, Second Report,* Law Com. No. 69 (1975); *Wathes (Western) Ltd.* v. *Austins (Menswear) Ltd.* [1976] 1 Lloyd's Rep. 14.

16 [1956] 1 W.L.R. 461.

17 *Mendelssohn* v. *Normand Ltd.* [1970] 1 Q.B.177, *per* Lord Denning M.R. at p. 182.

18 [1972] 2 Q.B.71. The clause in this case would be subject to a test of reasonableness before it could be upheld, even if it could be established to form part of the contract, under s.2(2) of the Unfair Contract Terms Act 1977.

19 In *British Crane Hire Corp.* v. *Ipswich Plant Hire Ltd.* [1975] Q.B.303 at p. 310.

20 [1956] 1 W.L.R. 461.

21 *Per* Denning L.J. at p. 467.

22 [1969] 2 A.C.31.

23 [1975] Q.B.303.

24 [1972] 2 Q.B.71.

25 [1956] 1 W.L.R. 461.

26   At p. 468.
27   *Cf. Roe* v. *Naylor* (1918) 87 L.J.K.B. 958 at p. 963 where it is pointed out that in that case there was no evidence that the terms in the note used on previous occasions had been the same and hence the condition in the sold note was not incorporated. See also *Butler Machine Tool Co. Ltd.* v. *Ex-cell-o Corpn. (England) Ltd.* (1977) 121 S. J. 406.
28   [1964] 1 W.L.R. 125.
29   At p. 134.
30   See *Henry Kendall & Sons* v. *William Lillico and Sons* [1969] 2 A.C.31; *sub nom. Hardwick Game Farm* v. *Suffolk Agricultural Poultry Producers Assn. Ltd.* [1966] 1 W.L.R. 287 (C.A.); *Hollier* v. *Rambler Motors (A.M.C.) Ltd.* [1972] 2 Q.B. 71, *per* Salmon L.J. at pp. 77-78; *Gillespie Bros. & Co. Ltd.* v. *Roy Bowles Transport Ltd.* [1973] Q.B.400.
31   In *Hardwick Game Farm* v. *Suffolk Agricultural and Poultry Producers Assn. Ltd.* [1966] 1 W.L.R. 287 at p. 339.
32   [1964] 1 W.L.R. 125; *Cf. Ashdown* v. *Samuel Williams & Sons Ltd.* [1957] 1 Q.B.409.
33   *Ibid.* at p. 138.
34   See *D.J. Hill & Co. Pty. Ltd.* v. *Walter H. Wright Pty. Ltd.* [1971] V.R.749.
35   See Cheshire & Fifoot, *The Law of Contract* (9th ed.), pp. 237-244. Spencer argues in [1973] C.L.J. 104 that a fourth defence to the signature rule, that of mistake, ought to be available.
36   He will still be able to argue, however, that he has not thereby assumed the risk of any negligence: see Unfair Contract Terms Act 1977, s.2(3).
37   [1934] 2 K.B. 394; Spencer [1973] C.L.J.104; see also *The Luna* [1920] P.22; *Blay* v. *Pollard & Morris* [1930] 1 K.B.628; *Saphir* v. *Zissimos* [1960] 1 Lloyd's Rep. 490.
38   At p. 403.
39   *Curtis* v. *Chemical Cleaning and Dyeing Co.* [1951] 1 K.B. 805; see also *Jaques* v. *Lloyd D. George & Partners Ltd.* [1968] 2 A11 E.R. 187.
40   Misrepresentation Act 1967, s.3; Sale of Goods Act 1893, s.55(3); Unfair Contract Terms Act 1977, ss.2(1), 5, 6(2), 7(2).
41   Sale of Goods Act 1893, s.55(4), (5); Unfair Contract Terms Act 1977, ss.2(2), 3(2), 4(1), 6(3), 7(3), 8(1), 11.
42   Clarke, "Notice of Contractual Terms" [1976] C.L.J. 51.
43   [1949] 1 K.B. 532; see also *Burnett* v. *Westminster Bank Ltd.* [1966] 1 Q.B. 742.
44   [1971] 2 Q.B. 163.
45   Such a clause would be void under the Unfair Contract Terms Act 1977, s.2(1).
46   At p. 169.

47   It is not clear that Lord Denning is correct in his analysis of the exact procedure of offer and acceptance in the case of automatic machines. Megaw L.J. at p. 170 expressed some doubt as to the "precise moment of time the contract was concluded" and there could be difficulties if, for example, the correct coinage was inserted into the machine yet, for some mechanical reason, it was rejected. If the offer is made by the machine, and that offer is accepted by the customer inserting his coin, then the proprietor of the machine will presumably be in breach if the correct coins are then rejected. The device of an invitation to treat has been created, as a matter of commercial convenience, to cope with such difficulties. Perhaps the correct analysis of the problem is to suggest that the machine makes an invitation to treat, the customer the offer, which is accepted by the machine receiving the coins and operating normally.

48   [1877] 2 C.P.D. 416.

49   *McCutcheon* v. *David MacBrayne Ltd.* [1964] 1 W.L.R. 125 at p. 129.

50   *Parker* v. *South-Eastern Railway* (1877) 2 C.P.D. 416; *Richardson, Spence & Co.* v. *Rowntree* [1894] A.C.217.

51   *Hood* v. *Anchor Line* (*Henderson Bros.*) *Ltd.* [1918] A.C. 837, *per* Viscount Haldane at p. 844.

52   *Thornton* v. *Shoe Lane Parking Ltd.* [1971] 2 Q.B. 163.

53   *J. Spurling Ltd.* v. *Bradshaw* [1956] 1 W.L.R. 461 at p. 466.

54   *Henderson* v. *Stevenson* (1875) L.R. 2 Sc. & Div. 470.

55   *Sugar* v. *London, Midland and Scottish Railway* [1941] 1 All E.R.172; *Richardson, Spence & Co.* v. *Rowntree* [1894] A.C.217.

56   *Stephen* v. *International Sleeping Car Co. Ltd.* (1903) 19 T.L.R.620.

57   *Burke* v. *South Eastern Railway* (1879) 5 C.P.D.1.

58   *Thompson* v. *London, Midland and Scottish Railway Co.* [1930] 1 K.B. 41.

59   *Saphir* v. *Zissimos* [1960] 1 Lloyd's Rep. 490.

60   [1930] 1 K.B. 41.

61   [1894] A.C.217. *Cf. Hitchman* v. *Avery* (1892) 8 T.L.R. 698.

62   (1877) 2 C.P.D. 416.

63   At p. 422.

64   [1940] 1 K.B. 532; see also *Mendelssohn* v. *Normand Ltd.* [1970] 1 Q.B. 177; *Burnett* v. *Westminster Bank* [1966] 1 Q.B. 742; *Taylor* v. *Glasgow Corporation* 1952 S.C.440.

65   *Watkins* v. *Rymill* (1883) 10 Q.B.D. 178; *cf. Walls* v. *Centaur Co. Ltd.* (1922) 122 L.T.242.

66   *Parker* v. *South Eastern Railway* (1877) 2 C.P.D. 416; *Harling* v. *Eddy* [1951] 2 K.B. 739 at p. 746.

67   Contrast *Parker* v. *South Eastern Railway* (1877) 2 C.P.D. 416, with *Alexander* v. *Railway Executive* [1951] 2 K.B. 882 at p. 886.

68   See *Adams* v. *Richardson & Starling Ltd.* [1969] 1 W.L.R. 1645; *quaere* whether a guarantee is a "contractual" document? See Ontario Law Reform Commission, *Report on Consumer Warranties and Guarantees in the Sale of Goods* (1972) Chap.3; Unfair Contract Terms Act 1977, s.5.

Chapter 3

THE STATUTORY CONTROL OF
EXCLUSION CLAUSES

There have been many attempts to control the operation of
exclusion clauses, or their incorporation into contracts, by
statute, and several different legislative techniques have been
used to secure this end.[1] However, these techniques all have
one characteristic in common — they all view exclusion
clauses as something apart from the other promises and
undertakings in the contract.[2] On one view an exclusion
clause is simply one form of incorporating into a contract a
statement of what the parties are promising, or not promising
to do—a negative statement delineating positive obligations.
All statutory attempts at control do not appear to acknowledge this and to a greater or lesser degree regard clauses of
exclusion as something separate from the promises and liabilities of the contract. Whilst this used to reflect the judicial
attitude also, the signs are that the judges are now taking a
different view of such clauses.[3] There is no such sign of a
change of direction in current legislative activity.[4]

A. *Total Invalidity*

Certain types of exclusion clauses are declared absolutely void
by statute. They are void either because the type of damage
for which they purport to exclude liability, or the contractual
duty the breach of which it is hoped to excuse, is such that the

public, consumer or commercial interest is thereby better served.

There are many examples of the former type. For instance, any provision attempting to negative or limit the liability of the operator of a public service road vehicle for death of or personal injury suffered by a passenger is void.[5] There is a similar provision in section 43(7) of the Transport Act 1962 to cover the carriage of passengers by rail so that a clause such as that held to be operative in *Thompson* v. *London, Midland & Scottish Railway Co.*[6] would now be of no effect. By way of further example, any antecedent agreement or understanding between the user of a motor vehicle and his passenger which purports to restrict the driver's liability to his passenger in respect of risks for which compulsory insurance cover is required[7] will be void under section 148(3) of the Road Traffic Act 1972. The matter is now brought under statutory control in a much wider form in that by section 2(1) of the Unfair Contract Terms Act 1977, a clause or notice will be void in so far as it purports to exclude or restrict liability for death or personal injury arising as a result of negligence. This provision does not apply, however, to the limited list of exceptions in paragraph 1 of Schedule 2 (see Chap. 4) nor to contractual limitations on liability which are permitted by international convention, or by a statutory enactment which extends provisions based on a convention to domestic carriage (s. 29).

An example of statutory voidness in respect of the latter type of exclusion is to be found in the Sale of Goods Act 1893. In their original forms, sections 13, 14 and 15 of the Sale of Goods Act 1893 contained terms to be implied, in the absence of contrary evidence, in all contracts for the sale of goods, dealing with such matters as correspondence of the goods to contract description, fitness of the goods for their purpose, the merchantability of the goods, and their correspondence with any sample. The original intention of the draftsman was to fill any verbal gaps left by commercial men in their agreements by means of implied terms.[8] The general tendency in the law of contract over the past twenty years to shift away from the protection of the commercial interest to the protection of the consumer interest has now resulted in the statutory insertion of compulsorily imposed terms as to quality by a redrafting of sections 12 to 15 of the 1893 Act.[9] Any attempt to exclude these terms in a consumer sale is now void.[10] Similar provisions apply to consumer hire-purchase agreements,[11] and to contracts which involve the transfer of ownership or possession of goods from one person to another or the use of expenditure of goods in the performance of any services, such as contracts of hire, exchange and contracts for work and materials.[12]

This technique of nullifying attempts to contract out of duties imposed by contract or legislation is becoming a common feature on our statute books.[13] It does, however, inhibit the reasonable bargains of reasonable parties, and creates extremely difficult points of interpretation. Where, for instance, in relation to section 13 of the 1893 Act, should one draw the line between a term that excludes a particular characteristic from the description of the contract goods and one which exempts the supplier from liability for supplying goods lacking that characteristic?[14] Such an approach also runs counter to the current judicial approach to contractual construction.[15] As will be shown later, there are grave dangers in treating exclusion clauses as if they had an existence completely independent of the promises and under-takings contained in the contract. For example, in relation to the implied undertakings as to quality in the Sale of Goods Act 1893 the position with regard to consumer sales com-pletely misses the basic point and function of exclusion clauses, which is the allocation of contractual risks or, put another way, who is going to pay if the goods are defective? The first priority under the legislation is the consumer and he is safeguarded in so far as any exclusion attempt by the retailer in relation to the statutorily implied terms will be void. However, the ultimate responsibility will in many cases be that of the manufacturer, yet whether or not the retailer can recover from the wholesaler or manufacturer depends upon the view the statute takes of exclusion clauses in non-consumer sales which depends, in turn, as we shall see, upon an element of judicial discretion. This applies without distinction between commercial sales in general, and commercial sales of consumer goods in the chain between the manufacturer, whose fault the defect may well be, and the retailer.

B. *The "Reasonable" Exclusion Clause*[16]

Some statutes have given to the courts the discretion to control exclusion clauses according to whether the clause is fair and reasonable. At the time of writing the law in this area is undergoing some modification. It is therefore proposed to deal with both the old and the new provisions. Taking the old first, under section 55(4) of the Sale of Goods Act 1893,[17] in all sales of goods other than consumer sales[18] any clause attempting to exclude sections 13 to 15 of the 1893 Act "shall not be enforceable to the extent that it is shown that it would not be fair or reasonable to allow reliance on the term." Section 55(5) lays down certain guidelines for the court to follow in deciding whether a clause is fair or reasonable. These deal with strength of bargaining position,[19] availability of alternatives (*e.g.* differential price quotations), the state of the parties' knowledge, reasonableness of time for complaints, and whether it was the acquirer who prepared the specification of the goods to be manufactured and supplied to him. The court must, of course, have regard to all the circumstances of the case and in particular the exact knowledge, actual or implied, that the buyer had of the extent of the term. More important, in practice, is whether the buyer freely chose to adopt the contract with the exclusion clause, *i.e.* whether the buyer could have obtained the goods from the seller or another source either without the exclusion at all or with one that would have been less unfavourable to himself.[20] The fact that the court can now specifically have regard to whether the commercial buyer obtained the goods on a "take-it-or-leave-it" basis or whether there was a true negotiation gives statutory force to the frequently expressed judicial pronouncements of Lord Denning M.R. in this context.[21] A party wishing to rely on a clause seeking to exclude the statutorily implied terms in a commercial contract may have to show that it has been arrived at by a proper process of negotiation and agreement.

A further example showing a similar approach is to be found in section 3 of the Misrepresentation Act 1967.[22] This enacts that any provision in an agreement which purports to exclude or restrict the liability of a contracting party for misrepresentation shall be "of no effect except to the extent (if any) that ... the court ... may allow reliance on it as being fair and reasonable in the circumstances of the case." The operation of this provision is rendered potentially more idiosyncratic and uncertain than section 55(4) of the Sale of Goods Act 1893 since there are no guidelines laid down for its application by the court. Value judgments in this area are notoriously subjective and the criteria for assessing whether a bargain is reasonably fair particularly uncertain,[23] although the courts are being increasingly asked to make such decisions.[24]

The section appears to apply to clauses excluding liability for misdescriptions, however trivial, but the usual commercial stipulations for a margin in, for example, specification of the goods would not be invalidated, either because there would be no misrepresentation at all if the deviation from specifications fell within the stipulated margin, or on the ground that such a provision did not exclude or restrict a liability or remedy, but merely prevented the liability or remedy from arising in the first place.

Professor Atiyah raises the interesting problem of the fate of an agreed damages clause under section 3 of the 1967 Act.[25] It is clearly a clause restricting liability and so prima facie does fall within section 3. However, as the members of the House of Lords observed in the *Suisse Atlantique* case,[26] genuine pre-estimates of damages differ from the usual types of exclusion clause in that they are inserted into the contract for the benefit of both parties, rather than just one of them. In *Overbrook Estate Ltd.* v. *Glencombe Properties Ltd.*[27] an arrangement whereby a principal limited the authority of his agent to make representations was held not to be a clause limiting or excluding the liability of the principal seller, and so not within section 3. Another type of case where there would appear to be no restriction or exclusion of liability or remedy which would otherwise arise may occur where the representor tries to evade the normal consequences of misrepresentation by stipulating that there should be no reliance on his statements, reliance being essential before it can be said that there is an operative misrepresentation.[28] For example: "The buyer warrants that he has examined the vehicle(s) and has not relied on any representation made to him by the seller, but solely upon his own judgement."

The operation of the exclusion clause is totally dependent upon the discretion of the court, which may not merely uphold or reject the clause, but uphold it "to the extent (if any) that the court finds it fair and reasonable in the circumstances." This appears to give the court a power to rewrite an exclusion clause altogether, perhaps by modifying an exclusion clause which prevents an award of damages or rescission by striking out the ban on damages and leaving the ban on rescission as being reasonable in the circumstances.

Aside from the existence of criteria as to reasonableness, there is one very significant difference between section 3 of the 1967 Act and section 55(4) of the 1893 Act. Under the 1967 Act the presumption is that the exclusion is void and it is therefore up to the party seeking to rely on it to prove that such reliance is fair and reasonable in the circumstances. Under section 55(4) of the Sale of Goods Act 1893 the exclusion is valid unless it is shown that it would not be fair and reasonable to allow reliance on it. This raises two difficulties. First, the buyer will have to prove a negative. Secondly, suppose the seller is in breach of the implied term as to correspondence with description under section 13 of the 1893 Act and he has attempted to exclude liability for breaches of such an implied term in the contract. It is arguable that the exclusion clause comes within the terms both of section 3 of the Misrepresentation Act 1967 and section 55(4) of the Sale of Goods Act 1893.[29] It will thus at the same time be both prima facie of "no effect" under section 3 and prima facie valid under section 55(4). The clause may consequently be upheld by the court under section 55(4), yet be declared of no effect under section 3 because of the differing burdens of proof. A most curious state of affairs that does not bring clarity to this area of the law. Notwithstanding this, however, the concept of the "reasonable" exclusion clause has been imposed on a new and very wide set of circumstances by the Unfair Contract Terms Act 1977.

1. *The Unfair Contract Terms Act 1977*

The Bill proposed certain changes in the existing statutory controls over exclusion clauses in contracts for the sale of goods, hire-purchase and related contracts in which terms are implied at common law, such as contracts of hire, exchange and for work and materials. Section 55, subsections (3) to (11) of the 1893 Act and section 12, subsections (2) to (9) of the Supply of Goods (Implied Terms) Act 1973 (dealing with hire-purchase) are repealed and replaced by similar provisions turning upon reasonableness which apply, by virtue of section 6, to contracts for the sale and hire-purchase of goods and by virtue of section 7 to the analogous contracts under which goods pass. As against a person dealing other than as a consumer, the statutorily implied terms in sales of goods or hire-purchase, or the similar terms implied by the common law in the analogous contracts for the supply of goods, can be excluded, but only in so far as the term satisfies a statutory concept of reasonableness. This statutory concept of reasonableness is now, however, in two parts, rather than one. There are still the criteria of reasonableness that were formerly found in section 55(4) of the Sale of Goods Act 1893. Now, however, by virtue of section 11(2) and Schedule 2, these apply all three types of contract under discussion and the considerations mentioned above in relation to section 55(4) of the 1893 Act apply with equal force to the identical provisions contained in the 1977 Act. However, whilst these special criteria of reasonableness now found in Schedule 2 to the Unfair Contract Terms Act 1977 must, by virtue of section 11(2), be had "particular" regard to, they must also now be viewed in the general context of reasonableness imposed by section 11(1).

2. *The general test of reasonableness*

Clause 11(1) adopts a general test of reasonableness in some way similar to that first introduced to the law by section 3 of the Misrepresentation Act 1967. It provides that the general reasonableness requirement is that the term must be a "fair and reasonable one to be included having regard to the circumstances which were, or ought reasonably to have been, known or in the contemplation of the parties when the contract was made." It is, however, now for the party claiming that the clause is reasonable to show that it is (s. 11(5)) rather than for the party challenging the exemption to show that it is not fair and reasonable. Since section 8(1) amends section 3 of the Misrepresentation Act 1967 so as to apply this new test of reasonableness to clauses excluding or restricting a liability or remedy for misrepresentation, the problems described above arising from the apparent conflict between section 55(4) of the Sale of Goods Act 1893 and section 3 of the Misrepresentation Act 1967 should not now take place.

It seems clear from the wording of section 11(1) that the test of reasonableness is to be applied taking account only of those circumstances which obtained or could reasonably have been anticipated at the date of the contract. The wording does not appear to admit of consideration of factors other than those reasonably known or in contemplation *when the contract was made*. There is no general power for the court to judge fairness and reasonableness "in all the circumstances of the case."

This must, from the businessman's point of view, since it is he, not the consumer who will be troubled by this provision, be the sensible course. It must be clear, or at least determinable from the outset, what each contracting party has agreed to do or to give or to abstain from doing. To quote the views of the Scottish Law Commission:

"It would be a considerable impediment to the undertaking of contracts involving plant of novel design or processes of a novel character if the party constructing the plant or developing the process were not in a position to ascertain in advance the range of obligations he undertakes. It would be impossible for him to ascertain the range of his obligations against a legal background where unpredictable circumstances subsequent to the making of the contract would be taken into account. It is no answer to say that, in practice, reasonable exemption clauses will not be cut down. A contracting party must be in a position to assess his risks before he enters into the contract, not only to facilitate his decision whether or not to insure against the contingencies which the contract involves or to establish an appropriate contingency fund. For the same reasons a solution should be preferred which enables a lawyer to give sound advice to a client who is contemplating entering into a contract. If such advice is not available, there may be unnecessary litigation which would inevitably involve delay and expense.''

As regards the test itself, this is to be applied, in addition to exclusion clauses in the contracts already discussed as falling within sections 6 and 7 of the Act, to clauses or notices exempting from liability for negligence (see Chap. 4), for breach in consumer or standard form contracts (see Chap. 6), indemnity clauses in consumer contracts (see Chap. 1), clauses excluding or restricting liability, or any remedy available, for misrepresentation (see s. 8(1)), and finally in the event of termination for breach (see Chap. 6). There are no criteria laid down for the court to consider in applying this general test (as opposed to the specific test for contracts of sale, hire-purchase and related transactions as contained in Sched. 2) and so its application is inevitably going to contain a strong subjective element. Whether such a provision will gain acceptance or support amongst the business community will depend, to some extent, on whether the courts choose to have regard only to the terms of the exemption clause or of the relevant contract, or whether they take account of the commercial and social realities of the situation.

The courts might, within the terms of the section, have regard to such factors as whether the bargaining position of the person against whom the clause is invoked was stronger or weaker than that of the person invoking it; which of the two parties it was more reasonable to expect to insure against the risk complained of; whether there was an option to take the contract without the exclusion clause, perhaps at an increased contract price and so on. Where the exclusion clause places a maximum financial limit on the amount the other party may recover, the reasonableness of the clause is made subject to two criteria (s. 11(14). First, the resources available to the *proferens* to meet the liability "should it arise," and secondly whether he was able to cover himself by insurance. It is impossible to evade the ban or controls on exclusion clauses by placing them in another or secondary contract (s. 10).

3. *Consumer and non-consumer dealings*

As will be seen elsewhere in this work, the "reasonableness" restrictions, generally speaking, only apply where an exclusion clause is pleaded against a person who dealt as a consumer. The notable exceptions to this are certain terms excluding liability for negligence where, except in the case of certain contracts of carriage, whether or not a person deals as a consumer is irrelevant, exclusions for misrepresentation and exclusion of the implied terms in sale, hire-purchase and the related contracts under which goods pass, where exclusion clauses are totally unenforceable against a person who deals as a consumer and subject to the reasonableness test when pleaded against a non-consumer.

It is incumbent upon a person claiming that a party does not deal as a consumer to show that he does not (Unfair Contract Terms Act, s. 12(3)). The definition of dealing "as a consumer" in section 12(1) of the 1977 Act follows closely the definition of consumer sale in section 55A of the Sale of Goods Act 1893. The "consumer" must not make the contract, or hold himself out as making the contract, in the course of a business and the party with whom he contracts must, conversely, make the contract in the course of a business. Where the contract is one of sale of goods, hire-purchase or related contract, the goods passing under or in pursuance of the contract must, in addition, be of a type ordinarily supplied for private use or consumption.

It will be noticed that this definition does not include the intermediate situation. The commercial buyer purchasing consumer goods for his own consumption but at the same time buying them "on the business" does not deal as a consumer. So, a mini-cab operator buying a car for his own use, or a doctor buying a car for his practice would not be within the terms of a definition. Nor would a private consumer who requires a washing machine for use in his home but who decides his purpose would be best served if he buys a commercial model. The fact that the goods are not of a type ordinarily supplied for private use or consumption would prevent the dealing being a consumer dealing. It is provided, by section 12(2), that a buyer at auction or by competitive tender may not, in any circumstances, be regarded as dealing as a consumer.

4. *Business activities*

The main provisions of the Unfair Contract Terms Act 1977 are designed to operate, both in relation to contract and tort liability, where that liability arises from breach of obligations or duties as a result of things done or to be done by a person in the course of a business (which need not necessarily be his own business) or from the occupation of business premises (s. 1(3). However, "business" in this context is given a wide definition by section 14. It is not confined to purely commercial activities but extends to the activities of the professions, government departments, local authorities and other public authorities, such as the statutory undertakings. There is, however, one notable exception to the general principle of excluding purely "domestic" arrangements from the operation of the Act. If the contract is one for the sale or hire-purchase of goods, then, insofar as the Act purports to affect certain liabilities which may arise as a result of the statutorily implied terms, these will include *any* liabilities, not just those arising pursuant to a contract entered into by one party by way of business.

5. *Judicial approval*

The Sale of Goods Act 1893 and the Unfair Contract Terms Act 1977 confer, as we have seen, a power on the Court to supervise the operation of the exclusion clause to the extent of deciding whether it is fair or reasonable. Another statutory device for producing the same result depends upon the court having to approve the incorporation of the clause into the contract *ab initio*, instead of simply pronouncing upon its reasonableness *ex post facto*. The former approach has the disadvantage that until the parties are in dispute, the court does not get the opportunity to pronounce on the reasonableness of the clause, by which time it may already have had the desired effect both on the contract price and on the conduct of the parties during the non-contentious operation of the agreement. The latter approach requires the court to sanction the clause *before* the contract becomes operative. So, for instance, under sections 32 and 33 of the Housing Act 1961, any lease or tenancy of a dwelling for less than seven years granted after November 24, 1961, provided normally that it is not protected as a business or agricultural tenancy, contains by virtue of those sections an implied covenant by the lessor to keep in repair the structure, exterior and installation for water, gas and electricity supply, for sanitation and for space and water heating. Contracting out is only permitted insofar as the County Court may exclude or modify the implied obligation if it thinks fit and both parties agree.[30]

6. *Administrative supervision*

Sometimes the supervision of "contracting-out" provisions will be left to an administrative agency, rather than the court. So, under section 11 of the Redundancy Payments Act 1965 the Minister may by order exempt certain employees from the protection of the Act where he thinks fit, in the case of a joint application of the parties to any agreement making provision for voluntary payments to employees on termination of the contracts of employment. The Act does not expressly require the Minister to satisfy himself that the provisions of the agreement are as beneficial to the workers as the statutory scheme, but it is generally assumed that the Minister will not ordinarily make an exemption order unless this is so.[31]

A development of this administrative supervisory technique is to be found in the Fair Trading Act 1973. This Act, in a way not possible under the somewhat crude non-consumer sales controls in the Sale of Goods Act 1893, does enable distinctions to be made between the consumer and the commercial interest without regard to the *type* of transaction concluded.

The Act created a new post of Director-General of Fair Trading, who has the general duty to keep under review commercial activities affecting consumers, and in particular, commercial practices which may affect adversely the interests of consumers in the United Kingdom.[32] The Act also sets up a Consumer Protection Advisory Committee,[33] to which may be referred various consumer trade practices, with a view to considering whether they adversely affect the economic interests of consumers.[34] These practices include practices affecting the terms and conditions on which goods or services are supplied, advertising of those terms and conditions, promotion of goods and services, methods of salesmanship, the way in which the goods are packed or otherwise "got up" for supply, and methods of demanding or securing payment.[35] So, in relation to exclusion clauses the practices covered by the Act include not only the substance of the clause but also its manner of incorporation into the contract. Where the Director-General of Fair Trading is of the opinion that the practice has the effect of misleading consumers as to their rights and obligations (for example leading them to believe an invalid exclusion clause is binding), or of subjecting them to undue pressure, or of causing inequitable terms or conditions to be imposed in consumer transactions, he may refer to the Advisory Committee proposed recommendations to prohibit or regulate the practice.[36] Following the Report of the Advisory Committee an Order may be made by the Secretary of State in accordance with specified procedure, subject to approval by both Houses of Parliament. Such an Order may contain such provision as the Secretary of State considers appropriate for giving effect to the proposals referred to the Advisory Committee, subject to any modifications proposed in the Report.[37] Contravention of the Order results in criminal sanctions,[38] and so one can foresee a situation in which continued use of an exemption clause could result in the commission of a criminal offence. Indeed, the first Report of the Advisory Committee has proposed that an Order should be made prohibiting the use of advertisements or written clauses which contain void exemption clauses (*e.g.* a notice declaring: "No Money Refunded"), which may mislead consumers who do not appreciate that the clauses are indeed void.[39] Such an Order has now been made.[40]

Under section 26 of the Act a contract is not rendered void or unenforceable only as a result of a contravention of an Order, so that imposing criminal sanctions on use of a particular term will not invalidate the whole contract, the other provisions of which may be enforced by the supplier. However, since the exclusion clause itself is illegal, the supplier frequently cannot rely on the clause as a defence in civil proceedings.

Additional functions are conferred on the Director-General by Part III of the Act which enables the Director to investigate business practices detrimental or unfair to consumers which have been persisted in by a supplier. The Director may require satisfactory written assurances that the practice will be discontinued. If such an assurance is not given, he may take proceedings before the Restrictive Practices Court to restrain the conduct.[41] For this purpose "unfair" covers breaches of both the criminal and civil law,[42] and will therefore include the use of practices, including exemption clauses, which are made criminal as a result of the Secretary of State's Order.[43]

C. *Statutorily Imposed Exclusion Clauses*

In a few instances exemption or exclusion from liability will be statutorily imposed into contracts. Where this is done the statute will also normally prohibit any further limitations of liability over and above the statutory provisions. So, the liability of a shipowner for goods exported from the United Kingdom is governed by the Carriage of Goods by Sea Act 1971,[44] which applies to all outward shipments under bills of lading, except for a few minor exceptions, and the parties cannot contract out.[45] The responsibilities of the shipowner in respect of the safety of the goods entrusted to his care are described in detail in the Hague Rules, Art.111, which are appended to the 1971 Act by means of the Schedule. The principle underlying the provision in Art.111 is that the shipowner is only liable if acting negligently, but the responsibilities of the shipowner under the Act are *lighter* than they are at common law,[46] and this is then compensated for by a provision that no contracting out is permitted. In those cases where the 1971 Act applies, the Rules further provide maximum limits for the shipowner's liability for damage to or loss of the goods shipped. These maximum limits of liability may be increased (but not decreased) by agreement of the parties or by a declaration of the nature and value of the shipped goods by the shipper before shipment, together with insertion of this declaration in the bill of lading.[47]

It is in theory possible for exclusion clauses to find their way into agreements as a result of the Fair Trading Act 1973, already discussed, though it must be admitted that the practical likelihood of such a thing happening seems exceedingly remote. The Director-General of Fair Trading may include in his recommendations to the Advisory Committee proposals relating to any matters mentioned in Schedule 6 to the Act. These include the prohibition of exclusion clauses but also envisage the imposition of a requirement that specified terms be *included*. These prohibitions or requirements may be incorporated in the Secretary of State's Order. It is conceivable, therefore, that the Director-General would, as a corollary to the imposition of certain statutory obligations, also recommend the compulsory inclusion of certain limitations on liability on one or other side of a consumer transaction.

In a different way the Sale of Goods Act 1893 imposes a limitation of liability on the parties in that in one case they are not permitted their own exclusion clause but, if any reduction in liability on the part of the seller is required, the statutory one only may be used. Section 1 of the Supply of Goods (Implied Terms) Act 1973 contains a redrafting of section 12 of the 1893 Act. The new sections 12(1) implies into every contract of sale of goods, other than one to which subsection (2) applies, an undertaking in the form of a condition by the seller than he has, or will have at the time when the property is to pass, a good right to sell. It further implies a warranty of quiet possession and a warranty that the goods are free from encumbrances. Section 12(2) now applies where it can be inferred from the circumstances of the contract, or where it is expressly stated, that the seller only undertook to sell such title as he, or some named third party, might have. It implies a warranty on the part of the seller that all charges or encumbrances known to him but not known to the buyer have been disclosed before the sale. There is a further implied warranty of quiet possession against disturbance by the seller, any third person whose title the seller has purported to transfer, and any person claiming title through or under the seller or that third person, subject to encumbrances already disclosed or known.

There was formerly doubt as to whether the operation of

the old (unamended) section 12 could be excluded by contrary agreement.[48] This doubt may itself have discouraged the draftsmen of standard-form agreements from attempting to exclude section 12 at all. The new section 12 gives the draftsmen an alternative. Whilst no doubt the intention of the new section 12(2) is to enable sellers to dispose of goods the title to which is insecure, one is forced to wonder whether sellers are, as a general rule, going to adopt the less potent warranty in the new section 12(2) in every standard form sale agreement.[49] There would seem to be nothing to prevent this and the buyer will, of course, always be the sufferer.[50]

Contracting out of section 12 altogether is prohibited in that any term attempting to exclude the implied undertaking is void. So, either the condition of good right to sell and the warranties for quiet possession and freedom from encumbrances apply, or the warranties in section 12(2) apply.[51] It is not possible to exclude both groups. The problem arises, however, when an attempt is made to exclude both undertakings. Leaving aside problems of breach of a fundamental term, which are considered later, which of the two sets of undertakings is the court to imply into the contract having declared the exclusion void? Presumably the normal implication would be the undertakings in section 12(1), but these are not to be implied if it appears from the contract or is to be inferred from the circumstances that the lesser obligations of section 12(2) are to apply. The parties clearly intend no obligation to be imposed at all but if that is impossible their intention is presumably to take the next best thing, *i.e.* the limited obligations of section 12(2). However, if the exclusion is void will the courts still have regard to it? If they do not, then there may well be nothing in the contract or the circumstances surrounding it to indicate that the parties intended anything but section 12(1) to apply. The result will, therefore, in some cases be the very opposite of what which the parties intended and, in commercial sales, insured against. This is one further example of the distortion to bargains that results from treating an exclusion clause as something separate and distinct from the "obligation-defining" terms of the contract.

Notes

1 See Treitel, *The Law of Contract* (4th ed.), pp. 161-165; *cf.* Uniform Commercial Code, art. 2-302; Spanogle, "Analysing Unconscionability Problems," 117 Pa. L. Rev. 931 (1969); see also *Williston on Sales* (4th ed. 1973), Chap. 11; Eorsi, "Exemption Clauses" (1975) 23 A.J. Comp.L. 215.

2 See Coote, *Exception Clauses*, pp. 1-18, and also *post*, Chap. 7.

3 See *post*, pp. 74-79, and also *Kenyon, Son & Craven* v. *Baxter Hoare & Co.* [1971] 1 W.L.R. 519; *Trade & Transport Inc.* v. *Iino Kaium Kaisha* [1973] 1 W.L.R.210; *Wathes (Western)* v. *Austins (Menswear)* [1976] 1 Lloyd's Rep.14; *Levison* v. *Patent Steam Carpet Cleaning Co.* [1977] 3 W.L.R. 90.

4 Unfair Contract Terms Act 1977.

5 Road Traffic Act 1960, s.151; see also Unfair Contract Terms Act 1977, s.2.

6 [1930] 1 K.B.41; *ante*, p. 46.

7 See Road Traffic Act 1972, s.143.

8 Chalmers, "Codification of Mercantile Law" (1903) 19 L.Q.R. 10.

9 Supply of Goods (Implied Terms) Act 1973, ss.2 and 3; and Consumer Credit Act 1974, s.192(3)(*a*) and Sched. 4, para.3.

10 Unfair Contract Terms Act 1977, s.6(2)(*a*), replacing the earlier Sale of Goods Act provisions: Sale of Goods Act 1893, s.55(7), as inserted by Supply of Goods (Implied Terms) Act 1973, s.4.

11 Unfair Contract Terms Act 1977, s.6(2)(*b*), replacing Supply of Goods (Implied Terms) Act 1973, s.12(3), as amended by Consumer Credit Act 1974, s.192(3)(*a*) and Sched. 4, para. 35.

12 Unfair Contract Terms Act 1977, s.7.

13 See also, *e.g.* Defective Premises Act 1972, s.6(3); Unfair Contract Terms Act 1977.

14 For an analgous example, see *Overbrooke Estates Ltd.* v. *Glencombe Properties Ltd.* [1974] 1 W.L.R. 1335; Coote [1975] C.L.J.17.

15 *Ante*, fn. 3.

16 See Leff, "Unconscionability and the Code: The Emperor's New Clause," 115 U. Pa.L.Rev. 485 (1967); Ellinghaus, "In Defense of Uncon-

scionability,'' 78 Yale L.J.757 (1969); Waddams, ''Unconscionability in Contracts'' (1976) 39 M.L.R. 369.

17   As substituted by the Supply of Goods (Implied Terms) Act 1973, s.4.

18   Similar rules apply to hire-purchase agreements; Supply of Goods (Implied Terms) Act 1973, s.12, as amended by Consumer Credit Act 1974, s.192(3)(*a*) and Sched.4, para. 35. Certain international sales are excluded: Supply of Goods (Implied Terms) Act 1973, s.6.

19   Assistance may be derived from such cases as *A. Schroeder Music Publishing Co. Ltd.* v. *Macaulay* [1974] 1 W.L.R. 1308.

20   Several of the manufacturers canvassed in the writer's survey said that, since 1973, they offer their customers the choice of the goods with, or without the exclusion clauses in their conditions of sale, a higher price being charged where the exclusion clauses are deleted.

21   See, *e.g. Thornton* v. *Shoe Lane Parking Ltd.* [1971] 2 Q.B. 163; *Gillespie Bros. & Co. Ltd.* v. *Roy Bowles (Transport) Ltd.* [1973] 1 Q.B.400.

22   See Atiyah and Treitel (1967) 30 M.L.R. 369; Treitel [1967] J.B.L.200.

23   Leff, 115 U. Pa.L.Rev.485; *cf. Campbell Soup Co.* v. *Wentz,* 172F. 2d.80 (3rd Cir., 1948).

24   See the provision in Consumer Credit Act 1974, ss.137-140 dealing with extortionate credit bargains.

25   Atiyah, *The Sale of Goods* (5th ed.), p. 129.

26   [1976] A.C.361; see *post*, Ch. 5.

27   [1974] 1 W.L.R. 1335.

28   *Jennings* v. *Broughton* (1854) 5 D.M. & G.126.

29   For the view that a statement cannot be both a misrepresentation and a term, see Cheshire & Fifoot, *Law of Contract* (19th ed.), pp. 262-263.

30   See also Law of Property Act 1925, s.84(1), as amended by Lands Tribunal Act 1949, s.1(4)(*a*); Housing Act 1957, s.165; Israeli Standard Contracts Law 1964, s.10. For a discussion of the advantages and disadvantages of this system see Law Com. No. 69 (1975), paras. 290-314.

31   See Hepple and O'Higgins, *Individual Employment Law,* p. 158.

32   Fair Trading Act 1973, s.2.

33   *Ibid.* s.3.

34   *Ibid.* s.13; see also Consumer Credit Act 1974, Pts. I & III.

35   *Ibid.* s.13.

36   *Ibid.* s.17.

37   *Ibid.* s.22.

38   *Ibid.* s.23.

39   See *Rights of Consumers: A Report on Practices Relating to the Purported Exclusion of Inalienable Rights of Consumer and Failure to Explain their Existence*, (1974/5; H.C.6), Report of Consumer Protection Advisory Committee, H.M.S.O. 1974.

40 Consumer Transactions (Restrictions on Statements) Order 1976.
41 Fair Trading Act 1973, ss. 35, 37.
42 *Ibid.* s.34(2), (3).
43 For a useful review of the arguments for and against the *prior* vetting and validation of exclusion clauses, see *Second Report on Exemption Clauses*, Law Com. No. 59, paras. 290-314.
44 See also Carriage by Air Act 1961, Sched. 1, arts. 22, 23(1) and 32; Carriage of Goods by Road Act 1965, Sched., arts. 23, 41; Carriage by Railway Act 1972, Sched., arts. 6(2), 7 and 10; Carriage of Passengers by Road Act 1974, Sched., arts. 13, 16 and 23(1).
45 Carriage of Goods by Sea Act 1971, Sched., art. 111(8). These provisions are unaffected by the Unfair Contract Terms Act 1977.
46 Scrutton, *Charter Parties* (18th ed.), pp. 198-205.
47 *Pendle & Rivet Ltd.* v. *Ellerman Lines Ltd.* (1927) 33 Com.Cas. 70.
48 See, *e.g.* Atiyah, *Sale of Goods* (4th ed.), p. 48; Guest (1961) 77 L.Q.R.98; Hudson (1957) 20 M.L.R. 236 and (1961) 24 M.L.R. 690; Samek (1959) 33 A.L.J.392 and (1961) 35 A.L.J. 437; Reynolds (1963) 79 L.Q.R. 534.
49 An examination of some standard form conditional sale and credit sale agreements used by large retailers and finance houses in the north-west of England seems to indicate that this is so.
50 The aircraft industry in Bristol, for instance, appears always to use s.12(2) rather than s.12(1) in its sale agreements. Most aircraft are used abroad as well as at home, where possible unintentional patent infringements in a complex piece of engineering would result in a plane being grounded, the loss for which could be passed back to the manufacturer (see *Microbeads A.G.* v. *Vinhurst Road Markings* [1975] 1 W.L.R.218) as a very expensive claim under s.12(1) of the 1893 Act.
51 Sale of Goods Act 1893, s.55(3), now replaced by the Unfair Contract Terms Act 1977, s.6(1)(*a*). There are similar provisions covering hire-purchase. In the case of the analogous contracts under which goods pass, s.7(4) provides that exclusion of liability in respect of the right to transfer ownership of the goods or give possession, or the assurance of quiet possession given to a person taking the goods under the contract, is subject to the test of reasonableness.

Chapter 4

THE CONSTRUCTION OF EXCLUSION CLAUSES

Once it is established that an exclusion clause has been effectively incorporated into the contract and that there are no
statutory provisions that affect its validity, it is then necessary
to determine exactly what the clause means. Before its operation can be finally analysed it is necessary to ascertain which
remedies the clause is purporting to deny, or of which
contractual duties it is attempting to relieve performance, and
so on. In other words the exclusion clause must be construed
so as to determine its impact on the obligations undertaken by
the contract as a whole. This raises the first of many problems
in this area: to what extent, in construing an exemption
clause, are the other terms of the contract relevant? Is the
exclusion clause merely a shield to a claim for damages, in
which case its construction will be a matter totally separate
from the rest of the contract, or is it instead just another
means, along with all the other terms of the contract, of
delimiting the extent of the obligations undertaken by the
agreement?

A. *Defence or Definition?*[1]

The real issue, then, is whether an exclusion clause operates
simply as a defence to breaches of the obligations of the contract, as determined apart from the exclusion clause, or
whether the clause has a part to play in defining these

obligations in the first place. The conventional view of both the majority of the judiciary and the legislative draftsmen,[2] is that an exclusion clause operates as a shield to a claim for damages or repudiation. The duties of the promisor are ascertained by construing the contract in ignorance of the exclusion and, where there has been a failure to perform one or more of those duties, regarding that as a breach. The function of the exclusion clause is then to bar a claim based on such a breach. This view was put by Denning L.J. in *Karsales* (*Harrow*) *Ltd.* v. *Wallis* as follows[3]. "The thing to do is to look at the contract apart from the exempting clauses to see what are the terms, express or implied, which impose an obligation on the party."

There is, of course, a grave illogicality in such an approach. Why should it be that one clause of the contract should be ignored when construing the rest of the contractual document and then itself be given separate construction? Taken to its logical conclusion, it could result in a situation where, viewing the contract apart from the exclusion, the parties have created valid contractual rights and duties, and yet a construction of the separate exclusion clause makes those rights and duties unenforceable. For example, suppose the promisor contracts to sell a blue G.T. Brooklands 2,000 Special motor car, but provides in the written agreement that he accepts no responsibility whatever if the vehicle should be of a different colour, model, make and engine capacity and any statements made by the promisor as to these matters are not intended to be, and should not be, relied upon by the buyer. There seems no sense in a court holding that the vendor had promised to deliver a blue G.T. Brooklands 2,000 Special, but that if he delivered a green Triumph 1500 he would not be liable because the exclusion clause provided a defence. The simple fact is that the seller has not promised anything at all in respect of colour, model, make and engine capacity. He has merely promised to deliver "a car."[4]

On this analysis it is possible to deal with some exclusion clauses in a totally different way. A clause drafted in exceptionally wide terms would not now just be struck out as repugnant to the contract, leaving all the other terms standing and enforceable on both sides.[5] Instead it would be seen as a "bargain" in which one party had agreed to be bound to his side whilst the other party had promised to do nothing whatever. It thus becomes clear that what has been concluded is not a contract at all since one party provides no consideration. It is simply an arrangement at will.[6] To use the words of Lord Wilberforce[7]: "One may safely say that the parties cannot, in a contract, have contemplated that a clause shall have so wide an ambit as in effect to deprive one party's stipulations of all contractual force: to do so would be to reduce the contract to a mere declaration of intent."

In extreme (and one may say, obvious) cases of this sort, this has always been the attitude of the courts. For instance, unconditional covenants not to sue are taken as a release.[8] In *Firestone Tyre Co.* v. *Vokins & Co.*[9] Devlin J. was, *inter alia*, required to consider the effect of the London Lighterage Clause, which was a clause incorporated into contracts of carriage by barge on the River Thames, relieving lightermen of liability for every class of damage except loss arising from pilferage and theft of goods while in transit. It was argued by counsel for the lightermen that they should only be liable if the goods were not delivered if it could be shown that they had been stolen in transit. Devlin J. said[10]:

> "One must construe the clause in the light of the contract. This contract is a contract of carriage, whereby the goods we entrusted to the lightermen as bailees and as carriers, and prima facie, therefore, subject to any exceptions they may have in their contract, if they do not deliver the goods they must show that the goods were lost not through their fault or that they are protected by some exception. If the

construction which [counsel for the lightermen] pressed upon me is the right one, it seems to me that it is not a contract of bailment or carriage at all. One may test the point by considering the construction of the contract if the phrase about pilferage of goods were not there. The position then would be that the lightermen have said: 'We will deliver your goods; we promise to deliver your goods at such and such a place, and in the condition in which we receive them; but we are not liable if they are lost or damaged from any cause whatsoever.' That is not in law a contract at all. It is illusory to say: 'We promise to do a thing, but we are not liable if we do not do it.' If the matter rested there, there would be nothing in the contract ... ''

Until quite recently, however, the judicial attitude towards the function of exclusion clauses in the majority of contracts, where the illusory nature of the promises given was not so apparent, has been that displayed in the passage quoted above from the judgment of Denning L.J. in *Karsales* (*Harrow*) *Ltd.* v. *Wallis.* [11] There is now some evidence of a judicial change of heart. It was, perhaps, begun in English law by Lord Wilberforce in the passage already quoted from his speech in the *Suisse Atlantique* case[12] but the argument was taken up by Donaldson J. in *Kenyon, Son & Craven Ltd.* v. *Baxter Hoare & Co. Ltd.*(13) He there said[14]:

"Protective conditions are of three distinct types; namely, first, those which limit or reduce what would otherwise be the defendants' duty; second, those which exclude the defendants' liability for breach of specified aspects of that duty, and third, those which limit the extent to which the defendant is bound to indemnify the plaintiff in respect of the consequences of breaches of that duty. A condition which provided that a warehouseman should be under no obligation to take greater care of perishable goods than was

appropriate to imperishable goods, would constitute a
good example of the first category of protective conditi-
tions ... If, in such a case, the warehouseman takes such
care of perishable goods as would be appropriate had they
been imperishable and damage results, he will escape liability not because the clause exempts him from liability for
breach of contract ... but because there has been no breach
of contract.''

This is, so far as it goes, a refreshingly sensible approach.
However, it is difficult to see, in view of his explanation of
the first category, why Donaldson J. requires the second.
Surely an exclusion of liability for breach of duty is another
way of limiting the duty itself. As has already been pointed
out, there is no difference in terms of what has been contrac-
tually promised between saying: ''The vendor gives no undertaking whatever, contractual or otherwise, as to make,
model, colour or year of manufacture of the vehicle,'' and his
saying: ''The vendor shall not be liable for any error of description whatever.''

This point was made a year later by Kerr J. in *Trade and
Transport Inc.* v. *Iino Kaium Kaishi.*[15] The rather complex
facts of this case turned on whether the owners of a vessel
could terminate the charter on the grounds of the failure, on
the part of the charterers, to produce a cargo before the
expiry of a frustrating time, notwithstanding the existence in
the charterparty of a clause excepting the charterers from
liability for failure to provide a cargo in certain specified circumstances, including unavoidable hindrance. Although Kerr
J.'s judgment refers extensively to the doctrine of fundamental breach, which is discussed in detail in Chapter 6, it is
worth setting out his analysis at length since it is the best
judicial exposition so far reported of the approach this
Chapter has been attempting to describe. He says[16]:

"The Charterers' failure to load a cargo at any time could never be a breach, let alone a fundamental breach, if the failure to supply and load a cargo was due to unavoidable hindrances covered by Cl.2 [the exemption clause] of the charterparty. It is an impossible argument, and one which puts the cart before the horse, for the owners to say that the supply of a cargo is prima facie an absolute and fundamental obligation and that they can therefore get rid of cl.2 by treating the charterers' failure to supply a cargo as a repudiatory and fundamental breach, although cl. 2 expressly provides that such failure shall be no breach at all if due to unavoidable hindrances. The correct analysis is that under this charterparty the charterers did not undertake an absolute obligation to supply a cargo, but merely the qualified obligation to do so unless prevented by any unavoidable hindrances within cl.2."

Here, then, Kerr J. displays a willingness to define the extent of the charters' obligation by reading the obligation to load and clause 2 *together*[17]; that is, regarding the exclusion clause as a negative way of defining the promises in the contract. Such an approach will clearly have an effect upon the way the clause itself is construed, and although "there is already in existence an impressive array of interpretative devices for containing exception clauses,"[18] the justification for their rigorous imposition is in some measure reduced. There is no reason why they should be subject to different rules of construction from any other terms of the contract. This view, however, has yet to receive judicial acceptance and it is now necessary to examine these "interpretative devices" more closely.

B. *Strict Interpretation of the Clause*

In order to exempt himself from a legal liability under a

contract, it is necessary for a person to use the clearest possible words.[19] The clause must exactly cover the liability which it is sought to exclude. So, a clause excluding liability for breach of warranty will not cover breach of condition, and this will be so even where the term broken, although a condition, is treated as a breach of warranty by virtue of acceptance.[20] Further, exclusion of implied conditions and warranties will not exclude an express term,[21] nor will a clause excluding liability for "latent defects" be construed as excluding the implied condition as to fitness for purpose under the Sale of Goods Act 1893.[22]

To be effective, therefore, it is necessary for the clause, on its true construction, to cover exactly the event which has occurred. A useful illustration of this principle may be found in a case decided under section 15 of the Sale of Goods Act 1893, which deals with the conditions to be implied on a sale by sample. Section 15 provides:

"(1) A contract of sale is a contract for sale by sample where there is a term in the contract, express or implied, to that effect.

(2) In the case of a contract for sale by sample —
   (a) There is an implied condition that the bulk shall correspond with the sample in quality:
   (b) There is an implied condition that the buyer shall have a reasonable opportunity of comparing the bulk with the sample:
   (c) There is an implied condition that the goods shall be free from any defect rendering them unmerchantable, which would not be apparent on reasonable examination of the sample."

Where the sale is by sample as well as by description, it is an implied condition that the goods correspond both with the sample and with the description.[23] In *Nichol* v. *Godts*[24] the sellers sold "foreign refined rape oil, warranted only equal to sample." They delivered oil which did not answer the description of foreign refined rape oil. It was held that the exemption clause related only to quality, so that it might have excluded the condition now implied by section 15(2)(c). However, it could not be construed as also excusing the sellers from their duty to supply goods answering the description. Similarly, a contract that the goods are to be supplied "with all faults" will not assist a seller who supplied a bulk not corresponding with the sample, although it might be effective to exclude the condition implied by section 15(2)(c).[25]

Any clause, then, will be given the narrowest possible scope consistent with the intention of the parties. This has the consequence, for example, that an express warranty will be considered to have been given in addition to (and not in lieu of) any implied warranties, unless there are indications to the contrary. This was the rule at common law[26] and has now been given statutory effect in section 55(2) of the Sale of Goods Act 1893. On this basis, a guarantee or undertaking in a factory warranty would not oust the implied conditions of merchantability and fitness for purpose otherwise applicable.[27] Indeed, under the Unfair Contract Term Act the operation of exclusion clauses in guarantees is closely controlled. Under section 5 any contract term or notice contained in a guarantee of goods will be of no effect in so far as it purports to exclude liability for certain loss or damage. To come within the provision the loss or damage must arise from the goods proving defective while in consumer use, and must result from the negligence of a person concerned in the manufacture or distribution of the goods. Manufacturers and distributors are potentially liable under the principle in *Donoghue* v. *Stevenson*[28] for loss or damage caused by their negligence. Sometimes "guarantees" or "warranties" are issued, particularly by manufacturers (the clause has no application as between parties to a contract under which possession or ownership of the goods passes (s.5(3)) which attempt to exclude or restrict this liability. The effect of this section is to make void such exemptions as attempt to exclude or restrict liability for negligence. Goods are to be regarded as in consumer use "when a person is using them, or has them in his possession for use, otherwise than exclusively for the purpose of a business" (s.5(2)(*a*). The section, then, is only designed to operate in the consumer situation. The goods must be consumer goods, *i.e.* goods "of a type ordinarily supplied for private use or consumption," and the loss or damage must arise from the goods proving defective while in consumer use. So, a housewife who purchases a commercial model washing machine cannot rely on the provision since the goods are not consumer goods. A doctor who buys a car "on the practice" but uses it both for business and pleasure may take the benefit of the provision since the car is not used, or possessed, exclusively for the purposes of business. Section 5 (2)(*b*) provides that: "anything in writing is a guarantee if it contains or purports to contain some promise or assurance (however worded or presented) that defects will be made good by complete or partial replacement, or by repair, monetary compensation or otherwise." Where the exclusion is not in the form of a guarantee, but simply in the form of a notice or warning that damage might result, *e.g.* a notice that the goods are likely to cause injury, that notice will not, by itself, be sufficient to indicate the voluntary acceptance of any risk for the purposes of the principle of *volenti non fit injuria*, even when the notice is agreed to (s.2(3)).

C. *The Contra Proferentem Rule*

If there is any ambiguity as to the meaning and scope of the words used in a clause excluding or limiting liability the doubt is resolved by construing them against the party who has inserted them, and who is now relying on them, and in favour of the other party. So, in *Webster* v. *Higgin*,[29] in the course of negotiating a hire-purchase agreement for a second-hand car, the owner's agent told the hirer that, if he took the car, the owner would guarantee that it was in good condition and that he would have no trouble with it. The hirer signed a hire-purchase agreement which contained, *inter alia*, this clause:

"The hirer is deemed to have examined (or caused to be examined) the vehicle prior to this agreement and satisfied himself as to its condition, and no warranty, condition, description or representation on the part of the owner as to the state or quality of the vehicle is given or implied ... any statutory or other warranty, condition, description or representation, whether express or implied as to the state, quality, fitness or roadworthiness being hereby expressly excluded."

The vehicle turned out to be "nothing but a mass of second-hand and dilapidated ironmongery,"[30] The Court of Appeal held that the wording of the clause in the hire-purchase agreement was not sufficiently clear to abrogate the separate oral collateral agreement constituted by the offer of the guarantee and the signing of the hire-purchase agreement by the hirer. Wrottesley L.J. said[31]:

"I think it impossible to reconcile these two matters—on the one hand, the collateral warranty, and, on the other hand, clause 5 of the hire-purchase agreement [the exemption clause] ... I agree with counsel for the defendant when he submits that to see whether a clause like clause 5 in a subsequent written agreement excludes a previous agreement or a representation or condition clearly made and entered into, as this one was, the subsequent clause must be strictly and literally construed, and against the person who desires to rely on it."[32]

D. *Repugnancy*

As has been pointed out earlier in this chapter, one effect of construing the contract, *including* the exemption clause, as a whole, would be the demise of the device of construing the exclusion clause as repugnant to the main purpose of the contract in an effort to strike it down. Until this view receives wide judicial support, however, the repugnancy doctrine is still likely to be canvassed before the courts. In *Sze Hai Tong Bank Ltd.* v. *Rambler Cycle Co. Ltd.*[33] the sellers contracted to sell a consignment of cycles to buyers in Singapore. The bill of lading for the carriage of the cycles by sea to Singapore provided, in clause 2 that "the responsibility of the carrier ... shall be deemed ... to cease absolutely after [the goods] are discharged" from the ship. The goods were discharged from the ship at Singapore and were placed in go-downs of the Singapore Harbour Board. There was a further obligation in the bill of lading that the goods were to be delivered at Singapore to the order of the sellers. On the order of the agents of the carriers the goods were released to the buyers, an indemnity being given to the carriers by the appellant bank. The buyers never paid for the goods. The appellant bank contended that the responsibility of the carriers ceased, under clause 2 of the bill of lading, when the goods were delivered to the buyers without payment and that, therefore, the bank was not liable on its contract of indemnity. Lord Denning, delivering the opinion of the Privy Council, said this[34]:

> "The exemption, on the face of it, could hardly be more comprehensive, and it is contended that it is wide enough to absolve the shipping company from responsibility for the act of which the respondents complain, that is to say, the delivery of the goods to a person who, to their knowledge, was not entitled to receive them. If the exemption clause,

on its true construction, absolved the shipping company from an act such as that, it seems that, by parity of reasoning, they would have been absolved if they had given the goods away to some passer-by or had burnt them or thrown them into the sea. If it had been suggested to the parties that the condition exempted the shipping company in such a case, they would both have said: 'Of course not.' There is, therefore, an implied limitation on the clause, which cuts down the extreme width of it, and, as a matter of construction, their Lordships decline to attribute to it the unreasonable effect contended for. But their Lordships go further. If such an extreme width were given to the exemption clause, it would run counter to the main object and intent of the contract. For the contract, as it seems to their Lordships, has, as one of its main objects, the proper delivery of the goods by the shipping company, 'unto order or his or their assign,' against production of the bill of lading. It would defeat this object entirely if the shipping company was at liberty, at its own will and pleasure, to deliver the goods to somebody else, to someone not entitled at all, without being liable for the consequences. The clause must, therefore, be limited and modified to the extent necessary to enable effect to be given to the main object and intent of the contract.''

The remainder of the Privy Council's opinion is concerned with the doctrine of fundamental breach, but this passage, based largely on the doctrine of repugnancy as spelled out in the judgment of Jenkins L.J. some three years earlier in *Renton & Co. Ltd.* v. *Palmyra Trading Corpn. of Panama* [35] has been the basis for the striking out of several clauses of limitation and exclusion, largely under the guidance of Lord Denning,[36] in other cases. A recent example is to be found in *J. Evans & Son (Portsmouth)* v. *Andrea Merzario* [37] where a clause purporting to exempt a carrier from liability for damage to goods shipped on deck was struck out as being repugnant to a binding oral promise given by the forwarding agents that the goods would be shipped under deck.

E. *Important Terms*

The courts have always taken the view that the very clearest of language is necessary to exclude liability for important terms of the contract. That is so whether the term's importance is to be found and ascertained at the time the contract is made[38] or by reference to the seriousness of the consequences at the time of the breach.[39] The matter was put succinctly by Lord Wilberforce in the *Suisse Atlantique* case[40]: " ... It must be a question of contractual intention whether a particular breach is covered [by the exclusion clause] or not, and the courts are entitled to insist, as they do, that the more radical the breach, the clearer must the language be if it is to be covered."[41]

F. *Liability for Negligence*

In *Hall* v. *Brooklands Auto-Racing Club* Scrutton L.J. said[42]: " ... In my view, where the defendant has protection under a contract, it is not permissible to disregard the contract and allege a wider liability in tort." However, there is a significant difference between disregarding the contract altogether, and construing the contract closely to ascertain whether the "guilty" party has effectively excluded his tortious liability by means of contractual exemption clauses. Whilst it is possible for a clause to be drafted in such a way that it excludes tortious liability (usually for negligence) the usual attitude of the courts is that it is exceedingly unlikely that one party to a contract intended to relieve the other party from liability for negligence unless the clearest possible terms are used.[43]

As a matter of construction[44] the courts have established that unless negligence is the only liability to which the words could apply, general words of exclusion will have no application to negligence. So, where the clause is framed in general words, *e.g.* a clause exempting liability "for all damage," or "for loss or damage," it will first be necessary to establish whether the head of damage complained of could arise both as a result of negligence *and* of breach of a strict contractual duty, or whether it can only arise as a result of negligence. If it can only arise as a result of negligence, then a clause in general terms may protect against liability for negligence. The leading case is that of *Alderslade* v. *Hendon Laundry Ltd.*[45] The plaintiff sent some handkerchiefs to the defendants' laundry under a contract which limited their liability "for a lost or damaged article" to "twenty times the charge made for laundering." The handkerchiefs were lost. The question arose as to what particular head of damage the limitation as to "lost or damaged" articles related. The Court of Appeal held that the only duty in relation to the safe custody of the handkerchiefs was that the laundry undertook to take reasonable care of them, that is not to be negligent. So, if the handkerchiefs were lost, the only possible ground upon which the laundry could be held liable was that of negligence. That being so, any exemption clause that purported to limit liability for lost laundry must be intended to apply to liability as a result of negligence, since that was the only ground of liability for loss. Otherwise the clause would be otiose. Lord Greene M.R. said[46]:

> "Where the head of damage in respect of which limitation of liability is sought to be imposed by such a clause is one which rests on negligence and nothing else, the clause must be construed as extending to that head of damage, because if it were not so construed, it would lack subject-matter."

If liability for negligence is excluded successfully, the injured party has no right of action for negligence either in contract or in tort.[47]

However, even where the sole obligation is to exercise reasonable care the clause should, if it is to be effective, indicate that it is intended to exclude liability in all circumstances, including negligence. Otherwise it may be understood as a simple warning that the defendant would not be liable in the absence of negligence. Being a question of construction it will not inevitably be the case that if the only possible liability of the party pleading the exemption is liability for negligence, the clause will be effective. It is simply more likely that it will be. So, in *Hollier* v. *Rambler Motors (A.M.C.) Ltd.*[48] the plaintiff arranged for the defendants to repair his car and, whilst it was at the defendants' garage, it was damaged by fire. On at least two previous occasions, when using the defendants' services, the plaintiff had signed a form containing the words: "The company is not responsible for damage caused by fire to customers' cars on the premises. Customers' cars are driven by staff at owner's risk." The Court of Appeal held that there was an insufficient previous course of dealing to import the exclusions clause into the oral contract; but, in any event, the fact that the defendants were only liable for loss caused by fire when this was due to their negligence was not decisive. The clause was not so plain in its language as to unequivocally cover damage caused by fire due to the defendants' own negligence only. The plaintiffs therefore succeeded in their claim for damages.

If the head of damage can, on the other hand, arise concurrently in negligence and on some further basis not requiring proof of negligence, then the rule is that general words of limitation or exclusion will only operate on the strict contractual liability, leaving the tortious liability intact. In *Alderslade* v. *Hendon Laundry Ltd.* Scrutton L.J. expressed this principle thus[49]: "Where ... the head of damage may be based on some ground other than negligence, the general rule is that the clause must be confined to loss occurring through that other course to the exclusion of negligence."

The most frequently cited application of this dictum is the case of *White* v. *John Warwick & Co. Ltd.*[50] The plaintiff, who had hired a bicycle from the defendants, was injured when the saddle tipped up and threw him into the road. The plaintiff sued the defendants alternatively for breach of contract and in tort for negligence and was met by an exclusion clause in the hire document to the effect that "nothing in this agreement shall render the owners liable for any personal injuries to the riders of the machine hired." It was clear that damages could be claimed by the plaintiff, either on the ground of negligence, or for breach of the strict contractual duty to supply a machine that was reasonably fit for the purpose required. The Court of Appeal held that the exemption clause only protected the defendants against strict liability and not, therefore, against breach of the duty of care in tort.[51] Again, this is simply a rule of construction. Under it, it is more likely than not that a clause will be held to exclude strict liability only, although it may be effective to exclude liability for negligence as well, because, for instance, it is construed as an indemnity clause.[52]

Where specific and precise words of exclusion, as opposed to general words, are used, which make it clear that the clause is intended to exempt the person relying on it from liability in negligence, then effect must be given to it. Such words as, "will not be liable for any damage however caused,"[53] or "will not in any circumstances be responsible,"[54] or "shall be indemnified against all claims and demands whatsoever," [55] or "all merchandise is expressly accepted at owner's risk"[56] have all been held to indicate a clear intention to exclude liability for negligence. In *Rutter* v. *Palmer*[57] the plaintiff left his car at the defendant's garage for sale on terms that "customers' cars are driven by our servants at customers' sole risk." The car was being driven by one of the defendant's drivers when it was involved in a collision and damaged. It was held that the clause effectively placed the risk of negligence on the plaintiff and so his claim for damages failed.

The Unfair Contract Terms Act contains extensive provisions controlling the use of clauses or notices purporting to exclude liability for negligence. The Act's provisions do not apply to things done otherwise than by a person in the course of a business or as occupier of premises for business purposes (s. 1(3)), so in other "domestic" situations the common law rules are intended to apply. Negligence, in the context of the Act, means breach of a contractual obligation to take reasonable care or exercise reasonable skill, breach of a common law duty to take reasonable care or exercise reasonable skill, and breach of the common duty of care imposed by the Occupiers Liability Act 1957 (s. 1(1)). It does not cover any stricter duty, so there is no control under these provisions over exemptions from liability for breach of such duties as that imposed under *Rylands* v. *Fletcher*.[58] Of course, if the facts which give rise to liability under *Rylands* v. *Fletcher* also give rise to liability in negligence the clause exempting liability will come under control to the extent that it is relied upon to exclude or restrict liability for negligence.

In some circumstances, exemptions from liability for negligence are made altogether void. These are, first, any clause excluding or restricting liability for death or personal injury resulting from negligence (with certain savings for exemptions sanctioned by international convention), and secondly, certain clauses contained in guarantees as described earlier in this Chapter. In other cases (with certain exceptions for non-consumer contracts of marine salvage or towage, charter-parties of ships or hovercraft and contracts for the carriage of goods by ship or hovercraft, as described in Sched. 1) any clause purporting to exclude or restrict liability for negligence is made dependent upon the requirement of reasonableness, discussed at length in Chapter 3 (section 2(2)). So, before these new provisions can be applied to any clause, it must first be established that the clause was intended to exclude or restrict liability for negligence as defined in the Act. That question must needs be decided by the common law rules of construction derived from *Alderslade* v. *Hendon Laundry*[59] and the like authorities which we have just considered.

It may be apparent from the agreement that the party claiming under the agreement undertook the risk of loss as a result of negligence notwithstanding the absence of a clearly and precisely worded clause of exclusion. An undertaking that one or other party is to insure against certain damage arising as a result of negligence may be sufficient to pass the loss from one party to the other.[60] Further, an exclusion clause which is directed primarily to exclude liability in contract may nevertheless contain a warning sufficient to discharge the promisor's duty of care in tort, thus preventing any further liability arising. So, it may be that a sale of goods "with all faults" will be a sufficient warning in some cases that the goods are dangerous so as to prevent tort liability as for dangerous goods from arising.[61]

Under the provisions of the Unfair Contract Terms Act 1977 such devices must fail. Under section 2(3), warning notices and similar devices are deprived of any effect *per se* in tort, since it is provided that awareness or even agreement to a contract term or notice purporting to exclude or restrict liability for negligence is not of itself to be taken as indicating a person's acceptance of any risk. As far as insurance clauses or similar "indirect" devices for shifting risk are concerned these are now likely to be regarded as clauses excluding or restricting liability, and thus subject to statutory control, by virtue of section 13. This does not contain an exhaustive list of exclusion clauses within the Act but it does explain that a reference to excluding or restricting liability includes:

(a) the imposition of restrictive or onerous conditions on the creation or enforcement of liability (such as an obligation to give notice of loss within a specified time);

(b) the exclusion or restriction of remedies (such as a limitation of liability to a specified amount) or the imposition of any prejudice (such as a "blacklisting," or an obligation to indemnify a third party, which would also be caught in its own right under section 4(1);

(c) the exclusion or restriction of rules of evidence or procedure (such as a provision that a fact is to be conclusive evidence of another fact).

An undertaking, then, that one or other party is to insure might be brought into review under (a) above and would then itself be subject to the test of reasonableness.

C. *General Rules of Construction of Contractual Terms*[62]

In addition to the special rules of construction so far considered, there are certain general principles of contractual construction that apply as much to exclusion clauses as to other written terms of the contract.

1. *Plain meaning*

Words in a written contract will be given their plain and literal meaning, unless evidence is specifically adduced to show that the word is to be understood in some technical or special sense. The rule may not be applied where it would lead to absurdity or inconsistency with the rest of the agreement.[63]

2. *Ut Res Magis Valeat Quam Pereat*

Where words are used that are capable of two meanings the Court will give to them the construction which will make the instrument valid rather than void.[64]

3. *Expressio Unius Est Exclusio Alterius*

Where the written contract makes express mention of a certain thing, it will automatically exclude any other thing of a similar nature. So that, whilst use of general words such as "all the fixtures and fittings therein" will include all the fixtures and fittings in the property, where those fixtures and fittings are instead enumerated in the document, all those not specifically mentioned will not be included.[65]

4. *Ejusdem Generis rule*

Where general words follow an enumeration of particulars, those general words must be limited by reference to the preceding particular enumeration, and be construed as including only all other articles of the like nature and quality. So, where an exclusion clause in a charterparty relieved the carrier from liability to deliver if prevented through "war, disturbance, or any other cause," it was held that the words "any other cause" must be restricted to events of the same kind as war and disturbance, and would not, therefore, cover delay caused by ice.[66]

H. *The Onus of Proof*

In terms of the construction of exclusion clauses, the object of the exercise is generally to prove whether or not the act which it is alleged constitutes the breach, or the loss which it is alleged resulted from the breach, falls or does not fall within the ambit of the clause. The problem of who carries the incidence of the burden of proof can therefore be an important question and have a significant result on the outcome of the litigation.

The general rule is that the legal burden of proving all facts essential to his case normally rests upon the plaintiff.[67] However, there are strong suggestions in the cases and by various writers that considerations of public policy constitute

the decisive factor, and that the incidence of the legal burden
of proof will vary depending upon which set of facts are
essential to prove a party's case and this in its turn will vary
according to the different branches of the substantive
law.[68]

So, in bailment cases, for example, it is settled that, once
loss of the goods is proved, the bailee has the onus of proving
that the goods were lost without his fault.[69] The presence of
an exclusion clause in the contract can make little difference
to this principle since the onus will still be on the bailor, in the
first instance, to prove that he has not received the goods, and
it will then be up to the bailee to show that non-delivery falls
within the contractual exception. Denning L.J. said in
Spurling v. *Bradshaw*[70]: "A bailor, by pleading and
presenting his case properly, can always put on the bailee the
burden of proof." In other words the bailee is put to disproving negligence. In *Levison* v. *Patent Steam Carpet Cleaning Co. Ltd.*[71] a unanimous Court of Appeal reaffirmed
this general principle.[72] Lord Denning M.R. restated his
pronouncement in *Spurling* v. *Bradshaw* thus:

" ... In a contract of bailment, when a bailee seeks to
escape liability on the ground that he was not negligent or
that he was excused by an exception or limitation clause,
then he must show what happened to the goods. He must
prove all the circumstances known to him in which the loss
or damage occurred. If it appears that the goods were lost
or damaged without any negligence on his part, then, of
course, he is not liable. If it appears that they were lost or
damaged by a slight breach—not going to the root of the
contract—he may be protected by the exemption or limitation clause. But, if he leaves the cause of loss or damage
undiscovered and unexplained—then I think he is liable ..."

However, in other types of contract the presence of an
exclusion clause can make a great difference to the incidence

of the burden of proof. So, if a plaintiff claims damages from shipowners for breach of contract to carry goods safely, and the defendants rely on a clause exempting them from loss or damage occasioned to the goods by a peril of the sea, they must prove that the latter occurred and caused the damage in question; but, if the plaintiff relies upon a proviso to the exemption clause relating to negligence on the part of the defendants, the legal burden of proving negligence also rests on him. In the case of *The Glendaroch,*[73] in which goods were lost when the ship in which they were being carried foundered on a rock, Lord Esher said[74]:

> "The plaintiffs would have to prove the contract and the non-delivery. If they leave that in doubt, of course they fail. The defendants answer is 'Yes, but the case was brought within the exception—within its ordinary meaning'. That lies upon them. Then the plaintiffs have a right to say there are exceptional circumstances, in that the damage was brought about by the negligence of the defendants' servants, and it seems to me that it is for the plaintiff to make out the second exception."

In the later case of *Hurst* v. *Evans*[75] Lush J. held that, where an insurance policy against loss of jewellery contained an exception in respect of theft by the plaintiff's servants, it was incumbent on the plaintiff to negative loss from this cause. It is possible that this transposition of the onus of proof from defendant to plaintiff is the consequence of the application of public policy considerations in non-bailment cases. However, Bailhache J. refused to follow the case in *Munro, Brice & Co.* v. *War Risks Association.*[76] This case concerned an insurance policy covering the loss of a ship through perils of the sea, subject to an exception in respect of enemy action. He held that the defendants bore the legal burden of proving that the ship was lost in consequence of such enemy action, with the result that the plaintiffs succeeded on their claim as the ship had not been heard of after she set sail, and there was no evidence of the cause of her disappearance. Bailhache J. decided that the question of onus of proof depended upon whether the exclusion clause simply excluded particular classes of case from the promise which, but for the exclusion would fall within it, or whether the exclusion qualifies the whole scope of the promise. In the former instance, the onus is on the defendant to show that the plaintiff's case falls within the excepted class. In the latter instance, the onus is on the plaintiff.

Such attempts to lay down rules are not especially helpful since there is little difference between a clause construed to read: "The insurers shall be liable for loss except that which occurs in specific circumstances," and a clause which says: "the insurers shall be liable for loss arising from all causes other than those specified." A promise with exceptions can generally be turned, by an alteration of phraseology, into a qualified promise[77] and the question of the onus of proof does not so much depend upon these problems of form but upon the question of which solution will do the least injustice to plaintiffs and defendants, and that will frequently turn on which particular public interest needs the greatest safeguards in the transaction in question. For example, whilst it is clear that the Court of Appeal were placing the burden of proof on the bailee in *Levison* v. *Patent Steam Carpet Cleaning Co. Ltd.*[78] as a matter of precedent it is equally clear, from his pungent comments on standard form contracts, that Lord Denning M.R. at least felt that the public interest demanded that it should, at any event in consumer bailments, remain that way.

Notes

1 See Coote, *Exception Clauses,* Ch.1; see also Nicholas, 48 Tul. L. Rev. 946 (1974).
2 See Chap. 3.
3 [1956] 1 W.L.R. 936 at p. 940; see also *S.S. Istros (Owners)* v. *F.W. Dahistroem & Co.* [1931] 1 K.B.247, *per* Wright J. at pp. 252-253. *Cf. G.H. Renton & Co. Ltd.* v. *Palmyra Trading Corporation* [1957] A.C.149.
4 See Coote, *Exception Clauses,* pp. 4-14.
5 *Glynn* v. *Margetson & Co.* [1893] A.C.351; *Sze Hai Tong Bank Ltd.* v. *Rambler Cycle Co. Ltd.* [1959] A.C.576; Glanville Williams, "The Doctrine of Repugnancy" (1944) 60 L.Q.R.69; *Mendelssohn* v. *Normand* [1970] 1 Q.B.177; *J. Evans & Son (Portsmouth) Ltd.* v. *Andrea Merzario Ltd.* [1976] 1 W.L.R.1078.
6 Treitel (1966) 29 M.L.R. 546.
7 *Suisse Atlantique Societe d'Armement Maritime S.A.* v. *N.V. Rotterdamsche Kolen Centrale* [1967] 1 A.C.361 at p.432.
8 *Ford* v. *Beech* (1848) 11 Q.B. 852; *Thimbleby* v. *Barron* (1838) 3 M & W 218.
9 [1951] 1 Lloyd's Rep. 32; see also *Kelsall* v. *Taylor* (1856) 11 Ex.513, *per* Martin B. at p. 534; *Scott* v. *Avery* (1856) 8 Ex.487; *Elliott* v. *Royal Exchange Assurance Co.* (1867) L.R. 2 Ex.237; *Trainor* v. *Phoenix Fire Insurance Co.* (1892) 65 L.T. 825; *Rose & Frank* v. *Crompton Bros.* [1925] A.C.445; *Levison* v. *Patent Steam Carpet Cleaning Co. Ltd.* [1977] 3 W.L.R.90.
10 At pp. 38-39.
11 [1956] 1 W.L.R. 936. This approach has been frequently repeated by Lord Denning M.R., *e.g. Levison* v. *Patent Steam Carpet Cleaning Co. Ltd.* [1977] 3 W.L.R. 90.
12 *Ante,* p. 76. See also Diplock L.J. in *Hardwick Game Farm* v. *Suffolk Agricultural Poultry Producers Assn.* [1966] 1 W.L.R. 287 at p. 339 *et seq;* and in *Czarnikow* v. *Koufos* [1966] 1 Lloyd's Rep. 595 at p. 607; Kitto J. in *The Council of the City of Sydney* v. *West* (1965) 114 C.L.R.481, at pp. 495-496; Windeyer J. in *Thomas National Transport (Melbourne) Pty. Ltd.* v. *May & Baker (Australia) Pty. Ltd.* (1966) 115 C.L.R. 353 at pp. 385-386. See further Sellers L.J. in the *Hardwick Game Farm* case (*ante*), at p. 309 and Winn L.J. in *Gillette Industries Ltd.* v. *W.M. Martin Ltd.* [1966] 1 Lloyd's Rep. 57 at p. 68.
13 [1971] 1 W.L.R. 519; see *post,* Chap. 4.
14 At p. 522.
15 [1973] 1 W.L.R. 210.

16 At p. 230.

17 It is to be regretted that this approach was not urged upon the Court of Appeal with success in the later case of *Wathes (Western) Ltd.* v. *Austins (Menswear) Ltd.* [1976] 1 Lloyd's Rep. 14; Reynolds (1976) 92 L.Q.R. 172. See Coote (1977) 40 M.L.R.31. See also *Levison* v. *Patent Steam Carpet Cleaning Co. Ltd.* [1977] 3 W.L.R. 90.

18 Coote, "The Effect of Discharge by Breach on Exception Clauses" [1970] C.L.J.221, 238.

19 *Alison (J. Gordon) Ltd.* v. *Wallsend Shipway and Engineering Co.* (1927) 43 T.L.R. 323, *per* Scrutton L.J. at p. 324.

20 *Wallis, Son & Wells* v. *Pratt & Haynes* [1911] A.C.394.

21 *Andrew Bros. Ltd.* v. *Singer & Co. Ltd.* [1934] 1 K.B.17.

22 *Henry Kendall & Son* v. *William Lillico & Sons Ltd.* [1969] 2 A.C.31.

23 Sale of Goods Act 1893, s.13(1).

24 (1854) 10 Exch. 191.

25 *Champanhan* v. *Waller* [1948] 2 All E.R.724. See also *Robert A. Munro & Co. Ltd.* v. *Meyer* [1930] 2 K.B. 312; *Shepherd* v. *Kain* (1821) 5 B. & Ald.240. Exemption clauses purporting to govern the remedies available or the time within which they may be exercised will be subjected to the same strict treatment: *Szymonowski & Co.* v. *Beck & Co.* [1923] 1 K.B.457 (C.A.), affd. *sub nom.*: *Beck & Co. Ltd.* v. *Szymonowski & Co. Ltd.* [1924] A.C.43 (H.L.); *Vigers Bros.* v. *Sanderson Bros.* [1901] 1 Q.B.608; *Minister of Materials* v. *Steel Bros. & Co. Ltd.* [1952] 1 Lloyd's Rep. 87. See also Coote, *Exception Clauses*, pp. 150-156.

26 *Bigge* v. *Parkinson* (1862) 7 H. & N. 955.

27 See judgment of Lord Denning M.R. in *Adams* v. *Richardson & Starling* [1969] 1 W.L.R. 1645; see also *Western Tractor Ltd.* v. *Dyck* (1969) 7 D.L.R. (3d) 535, *per* Brownridge J.A. at pp. 543-544 (Sask. C.A.); *Sutter* v. *St. Clair Motors Inc.*, 194 N.E. 2d 674 (Ill.1963). Factory warranties may, notwithstanding this, stipulate that such "guarantees" are given in lieu of any other undertakings: see *Henningsen* v. *Bloomfield Motors Inc.* 161 A 2d 69 (N.J.1960); *Eimco Corp.* v. *Tutt Bryant Ltd.* [1970] 2 N.S. W.S.R.249.

28 [1952] A.C. 562.

29 [1948] 2 All E.R.127. See also *Lee (John) & Son (Grantham) Ltd.* v. *Railway Executive* [1949] 2 All E.R.581; *Harling* v. *Eddy* [1951] 2 K.B.739; *Adams* v. *Richardson & Starling Ltd.* [1969] 1 W.L.R.1645, *per* Lord Denning M.R. at p. 1653. See also *Couchman* v. *Hill* [1947] K.B.554, where a printed exemption clause was overridden by a later oral promise.

30 *Per* Lord Greene M.R. at p. 128.

31 At p. 130.

32 See also *Houghton* v. *Trafalgar Insurance* [1954] 1 Q.B.247; *Beck & Co.* v. *Szymonowski* [1924] A.C.43.

33 [1959] A.C. 576; see also *Suzuki* v. *Benyon* (1926) 42 T.L.R. 269 at p. 271; *Forbes* v. *Git* [1922] 1 A.C.256 at p. 259.

34 At pp. 586-587.

35 [1956] 1 Q.B.462 at p. 501 (C.A.); affmd. [1957] A.C.149 (H.L.). See also *Glynn* v. *Margetson & Co.* [1893] A.C. 351 at p. 357.

36 *E.g. Mendelssohn* v. *Normand Ltd.* [1970] 1 Q.B. 177 at p. 184; *Anglo Continental Holidays* v. *Typaldos Lines* [1967] 2 Lloyd's Rep. 61.

37 [1976] 1 W.L.R. 1078.

38 *E.g.* terms implied by law and classified *ab initio* as conditions, as under The Sale of Goods Act 1893, ss. 12-15. See *e.g. Goldsmith* v. *Great Western Railway* (1881) 44 L.T.181 at p. 182; *Clarke* v. *Army & Navy Stores* [1903] 1 K.B.155; *Rathbone* v. *MacIver* [1903] 2 K.B. 378 at pp. 383-384; *Bond, Connolly* v. *Federal Steam Navigation Co.* (1905) 21 T.L.R. 438 at p. 440; *McFadden* v. *Blue Star Line* [1905] 1 K.B. 697 at p. 705. See also Coote, *Exception Clauses*, p. 114.

39 *Hongkong Fir Shipping Co.* v. *Kawasaki Kisen Kaisha* [1962] 2 Q.B.26; *Harbutts Plasticine* v. *Wayne Tank & Pump Co.* [1970] 1 Q.B.447.

40 [1967] 1 A.C. 361 at p. 432.

41 See also Lord Denning M.R. in *Levison* v. *Patent Steam Carpet Cleaning Co. Ltd.* [1977] 3 W.L.R. 90.

42 [1933] 1 K.B. 205 at p. 213.

43 *Gillespie Bros. Ltd.* v. *Roy Bowles Transport Ltd.* [1973] Q.B.400 at p. 419.

44 *Archdale* v. *Comservices* [1954] 1 W.L.R. 459 at pp. 461, 463; *White* v. *John Warwick* [1953] 1 W.L.R. 1285 at p. 1293.

45 [1945] K.B.189.

46 At p. 192.

47 *The Albion* [1953] 1 W.L.R. 1026 at p. 1030; *The Kite* [1933] P.154; *Elder Dempster* v. *Paterson Zochonis* [1924] A.C.522; *Pyrene* v. *Scindia Navigation Co.* [1954] 2 Q.B. 402; *Smackman* v. *General Steam Navigation Co.* (1908) 13 Com. Cas. 196; *cf. Harbutts Plasticine* v. *Wayne Tank & Pump Co.* [1970] 1 Q.B. 447.

48 [1972] 2 Q.B. 71; see also *Re Polemis* [1921] 3 K.B. 560.

49 [1945] K.B.189 at p. 192.

50 [1953] 1 W.L.R. 1285; see also *Canada Steamship Lines* v. *The King* [1952] A.C. 292; *Badham* v. *Lambs* [1946] K.B.45; *Malfroot* v. *Noxall* (1935) 51 T.L.R.551; Gower (1954) 17 M.L.R. 155.

51 See also *Hawkes Bay and East Coast Aero Club* v. *McCleod,* [1972] N.Z.L.R. 289 at p. 308.

52 *Hair and Skin Trading Co.* v. *Norman Airfreight Carriers and World Transport Agencies* [1974] 1 Lloyd's Rep. 443.

53 *Joseph Travers & Sons Ltd.* v. *Cooper* [1915] 1 K.B.73; *Ashby* v. *Tolhurst* [1937] 2 K.B. 242; *White* v. *Blackmore* [1972] 2 Q.B.651.

54 *Harris Ltd.* v. *Continental Express Ltd.* [1961] 1 Lloyd's Rep. 251; *J. Carter (Fine Worsteds) Ltd.* v. *Hanson Haulage (Leeds) Ltd.* [1965] 2 Q.B. 495.

55 *Gillespie Bros. & Co. Ltd.* v. *Roy Bowles Transport Ltd.* [1973] Q.B.400; *A.E. Farr Ltd.* v. *Admiralty* [1953] 1 W.L.R. 965.

56 *Levison* v. *Patent Steam Carpet Cleaning Co. Ltd.* [1977] 3 W.L.R. 90.

57 [1922] 2 K.B. 87.

58 (1868) L.R.3. H.L.330.

59 [1945] K.B. 189.

60 *Archdale Ltd.* v. *Comservices Ltd.* [1954] 1 W.L.R. 459.

61 *Ward* v. *Hobbs* (1878) 4 App.Cas.13; see *Clarke* v. *Army & Navy Stores* [1903] 1 K.B. 155, *per* Romer L.J. at p. 166. See also Coote, *Exception Clauses,* pp. 34-36.

62 Professor Coote has suggested other rules that can be developed to construe exclusion clauses: see [1970] C.L.J. 221, 239.

63 *Abbott* v. *Middleton* (1858) 7 H.L.C. 68; *Watson* v. *Haggitt* [1928] A.C.127.

64 *Haigh* v. *Brooks* (1839) 10 A & E. 309; *Steele* v. *Hoe* (1849) 14 Q.B. 431.

65 *Hare* v. *Horton* (1833) 5 B. & Ad. 715.

66 *Tillmanns* v. *S.S. Knutsford* [1908] 2 K.B. 385; affmd. [1908] A.C.406.

67 See Cross, *Evidence* (4th ed.), pp. 73-92. This may, of course, be reversed by statute—see Misrepresentation Act 1967, s.2(2).

68 *Joseph Constantine Steamship Line Ltd.* v. *Imperial Smelting Corp. Ltd.* [1942] A.C.154; Stone (1944) 60 L.Q.R. 278; Cross, *Evidence* (4th ed.), pp. 84-85.

69 *Coldman* v. *Hill* [1919] 1 K.B. 443; *Brook's Wharf and Bull Wharf Ltd.* v. *Goodman Bros.* [1937] 1 K.B.534; *Houghland* v. *R.R. Low (Luxury Coaches) Ltd.* [1962] 1 Q.B.694; *Firestone Tyre & Rubber Co. Ltd.* v. *Vokins & Co. Ltd.* [1951] 1 Lloyd's Rep. 32.

70 [1956] 1 W.L.R. 461 at p. 466. See also *Hunt & Winterbotham (West of England) Ltd.* v. *B.R.S. (Parcels) Ltd.* [1962] 1 Q.B.617.

71 [1977] 3 W.L.R. 90. See also *Woolmer* v. *Delmer Price* [1955] 1 Q.B.291.

72 Lord Denning M.R. at p. 98; Orr L.J. at p. 98-99; Sir David Cairns at p. 100.

73 [1894] P. 226.

74 At p. 231; *cf. Slattery* v. *Manse* [1962] 1 Q.B.676.

75 [1917] 1 K.B. 352.

76 [1918] 2 K.B. 78; see also Devlin J.'s analysis of the problem in *Firestone Tyre & Rubber Co. Ltd.* v. *Vokins & Co. Ltd.* [1951] 1 Lloyd's Rep. 32 at pp.

38-39; *cf. William Soanes Ltd.* v. *F.E. Walker Ltd.* (1946) 79 Ll. L. Rep. 646.
77   See Devlin J. in *Firestone Tyre and Rubber Co. Ltd.* v. *Vokins & Co. Ltd.* [1951] 1 Lloyd's Rep. 32 at p. 38.
78   [1977] 3 W.L.R. 90.

Chapter 5

EXCLUSION CLAUSES AND THIRD PARTIES

It is an axiomatic principle of English law that a contract cannot, as a general rule, confer rights or impose obligations on persons who are not parties to it.[1] In particular reference to exclusion clauses this fundamental principle, one would have thought, would successfully prevent an exclusion clause affecting a third party, either as regards the benefit of the clause, or the burden of it. However, such a statement would be an over-simplification of the problem, as recent cases show.

A. *May a Third Party Take the Benefit of the Clause?*

This is a problem that arises most frequently in connection with the negligent performance, by an employee or agent, of his duties, pursuant to a contract between the plaintiff and the employer or principal which contains a clause exempting the employer and his employees or agents from liability for injury or loss caused in the performance of the contract. It is a principle of law that, as a general rule of agency, an employee is entitled to the immunities of his employer except where those immunities are by their nature personal to the employer. The basic rule is that acts are lawful if done by an agent acting within the scope of his authority if such acts would be lawful if done by the principal.[2] In the context of exclusion clauses this proposition became enshrined in a decision of the House of Lords in *Elder, Demptster & Co.* v. *Paterson, Zochonis & Co.*[3] In this case a company agreed to carry the plaintiffs' cargo of palm oil from West Africa to England and chartered a vessel for this purpose. The contract of carriage made between the plaintiffs and the company contained a clause of exclusion that purported to exclude liability, not only on the part of the charterers, but also on the part of the shipowners, for bad stowage. The shipowners were not, of course, parties to the contract of carriage made between the plaintiffs and the charterers. The barrels of oil were damaged by bad stowage and the plaintiffs sued both the charterers and the shipowners. The House of Lords held that the clause not only protected the charterers, but also the shipowners against the consequences of bad stowage, and the plaintiffs' action consequently failed.

The principle of "vicarious immunity" was established in the speech of Viscount Cave.[4] He said: "It may be that the owners were not directly parties to the contract; but they took possession of the goods ... on behalf of and as the agents of the charterers, and so can claim the same protection as their principals." So, it would seem that where a person employs an agent to perform a contract, that agent is entitled, in performing the contract, to any immunity from liability which the contract confers on the principal. The shipowners were therefore protected because they were the charterers' agents for performing the charterers' contract with the plaintiffs. The reasoning in this case has been criticised as being inconsistent with the doctrine of privity[5] but this is not the way to view the matter. The reasoning is perfectly consistent with the doctrine of agency. It is the law of agency itself that forms a useful and long-established exception to the doctrine of privity. This aside, the principle of vicarious immunity, albeit spelled out by Viscount Cave, appeared to receive the support of his fellow brethren[6] and, as Professor Coote has said, this statement of principle therefore "has the support of a unanimous House of Lords.''[7]

The principle was built upon one year later by Scrutton L.J. in *Mersey Shipping and Transport Co. Ltd.* v. *Rea Ltd.*[8] when he said '' ... where there is a contract which contains an exemption clause the servants or agents who act under that contract have the benefit of the exemption clause. They cannot be sued in tort as independent people, but they can claim the protection of the contract made with their employers on whose behalf they are acting.''

However, such a statement can be taken further. It must logically follow from Viscount Cave's promise that an employee acting as agent for his employer in carrying out his employer's contract is entitled to the benefit of any protection in that contract even though the exclusion clause may not expressly refer to the principal's employees or agents at all, and it ought also to extend to sub-contractors as well as to employees since they are just as much agents and thus entitled to the same protection as their principals.[9]

However, despite its firm foundations in agency, the principle of vicarious immunity was not well received. Reasons were found for not applying Viscount Cave's dictum in the case of contracts of carriage of passengers, both on land[10] and by sea.[11] Ultimately, on somewhat dubious grounds[12] and with the strong dissent of Lord Denning, the House of Lords rejected it in *Scruttons Ltd.* v. *Midland Silicones Ltd.*[13] In that case, a drum of chemicals was shipped to London from New York. The contract of carriage exempted the carriers from liability in excess of $500 per package. In the course of being handled during unloading the drum was damaged by the negligence of the appellants, a firm of stevedores employed by the carriers, and the damage done amounted to over three times the limit imposed by the contract. The respondents sought to recover the full loss from the appellants who, although not parties to the bill of lading, nor expressly mentioned therein, set up the limitation clause in defence. A majority of the House of Lords made a firm (though irrelevant) restatement of the doctrine of privity of contract and refused to find any general statement of the principle of vicarious immunity in the *Elder Dempster* case that could be binding upon them. Further, the House of Lords refused to hold the appellants protected on any other principle. There could be no implied contract between the respondents and the appellants incorporating the limitation by tacit reference, and the shipping company had not acted as agent of the appellants for the purpose of making the contract with the respondents. And further, a point which appeared to carry all their Lordships save Lord Denning, the limitation of liability only referred to "the carrier." It was not worded to cover their servants or agents.[14]

The effect of this decision was to open the door to claims in tort for negligence against individual employees or agents who, whilst acting within the scope of their employment or agency, act negligently with consequent injury to the plaintiff. Whether employers then compensate their employees for any damages awarded against them[15] does not affect the plaintiff's claim. However, the House of Lords did not appear to close the door to any form of exclusion from liability on the part of servants or agents, and indeed this is sometimes done by statute.[16] It was thought, however, that to be effective the clause must not only purport to be made on behalf of the employee or agent to be protected, but also purport to make him a party to the contract. It was even then doubtful that, unless the clause be contained in a deed,[17] it would be effective on account of the failure of the employee or agent to provide consideration.

The problems created by the *Midland Silicones* decision were recently reviewed by the Privy Council in *New Zealand Shipping Co. Ltd.* v. *A.M. Satterthwaite & Co. Ltd.*[18] where the great offence done to public policy and employer/ employee relations by the *Midland Silicones* case was to some extent remedied, although it is a pity that it required such a complex piece of drafting to do it.

In this case machinery was despatched from Liverpool to New Zealand. On arrival the machinery was damaged by the admitted negligence of employees of the stevedore while it was being unloaded. The consignors signed a bill of lading which contained a clause, sometimes known as a *Himalaya* Clause,[19] in the following terms:

"I. It is hereby expressly agreed that no servant or agent of the Carrier (including every independent contractor from time to time employed by the Carrier) shall in any circumstances whatsoever be under any liability whatsoever to the Shipper, Consignee or Owner of the goods or to any holder of this Bill of Lading for any loss, damage or delay of whatsoever kind arising or resulting directly or indirectly from any act, neglect or default on his part while acting in the course of or in connection with his employment and, without prejudice to the generality of the foregoing provisions in this Clause, every exemption, limitation condition, and liberty herein contained and every right, exemption from liability, defence and immunity of whatsoever nature applicable to the Carrier or to which the Carrier is entitled hereunder shall also be available and shall extend to protect every such servant or agent of the Carrier acting as aforesaid and for the purpose of all the foregoing provisions of this Clause the Carrier is or shall be deemed to be acting as agent or trustee on behalf of and for the benefit of all persons who are or might be his servants or agents from time to time (including independent contractors as aforesaid) and all such persons shall to this extent be deemed to be parties to the contract in or evidenced by this Bill of Lading ...

The Carrier will not be accountable for any goods of any description beyond £100 in respect of any one package or unit unless ... [there then follow arrangements for specifying value].''

Whilst admiring the comprehensive nature of such draftsmanship, it is only to be regretted that such complexity was required to achieve the desired end. The consignees of the goods, who had then become its owners, sued the stevedores who claimed the protection of the bill of lading. So, neither party to the litigation was a party to the original contract of carriage. As far as the plaintiffs were concerned, the New Zealand courts[20] held that the plaintiffs were placed in the shoes of the consignors (an original party to the contract), and therefore took over their contractual rights, by virtue of certain statutory provisions in the New Zealand Mercantile Law Act of 1908, making them subject to ''the same liabilities in respect of such goods as if the contract contained in the bill of lading had been made with'' them.[21] The Privy Council, on the other hand, preferred the view that by presenting the bill of lading and requesting the goods, the consignee offers to enter into a contract with the shipowner for delivery on the terms of the bill of lading.[22] On either view, however, the plaintiffs were treated as being in the same position to sue as the consignors would have been in had the bill of lading not been passed.

All the members of the Privy Council agreed that third persons, such as the stevedores, could be protected by an appropriately drawn clause and a majority held that the clause in issue did so protect them. Lord Wilberforce, delivering the majority opinion, said that[23]:

''There is possibly more than one way of analysing this business transaction into the necessary components ... the bill of lading brought into existence a bargain initially unilateral but capable of becoming mutual, between the shipper and the appellant [stevedores], made through the carrier as agent. This became a full contract when the

> appellant performed services by discharging the goods. The performance of these services for the benefit of the shipper was the consideration for the agreement by the shipper that the appellant should have the benefit of the exemptions and limitations contained in the bill of lading.''

Alternatively, Lord Wilberforce suggests that it may be that an immediate bilateral contract might have been concluded between the consignors and the stevedores through the agency of the carriers. In this case it was the agreement to unload, rather than the actual unloading, which was the consideration, and this is so even though the stevedores were already under a duty to the carriers to discharge the cargo. Lord Wilberforce said[24] that "an agreement to do an act which the promisor is under an existing obligation to a third party to do, may quite well amount to valid consideration and does so in the present case."

Aside from the technicalities of offer, acceptance and consideration, however, the decision granting the stevedores the protection of the clause goes a long way to restoring commercial common sense. No doubt the price of such exemptions is a lower freight rate and there is no sound commercial reason, or reason of justice, why the consignors should have the benefit of lower freight charges *and* an unlimited right of action for damages. This recognition is implicit in the majority opinion of the Privy Council and is to be welcomed for that. A rigid insistence on technicalities of the privity doctrine has allowed businessmen, dealing at arm's length, to evade the consequences of promises knowingly made.

This common law position is, to some extent, affected by the Unfair Contract Terms Act. By section 2(1), any attempt by reference to any contract term or notice to exclude or restrict liability for death or personal injury resulting from negligence (which is defined as a breach of the duty of care imposed both by the common law and by any contract) shall be void. This will be so even where the person or persons whose liability it is intended to exclude are not themselves parties to the contract. By virtue of section 1(2) and Schedule 1 this provision extends to contracts of marine salvage or towage and marine carriage of goods and charterparties. In the case of other loss or damage a person (whether a party to the contract or not) "cannot so exclude or restrict his liability for negligence except in so far as the term or notice satisfies the requirement of reasonableness." Although section 2(2) here appears to envisage the party causing the damage as actively attempting to exclude his own liability rather than passively having it excluded on his behalf by another, it is submitted that the better opinion is that this clause will nevertheless be subject to the reasonableness doctrine clauses that would, under the common law, successfully exclude liability on behalf of third parties.

It is provided in Schedule 1 that neither section 2(1) or (2) extends to a contract of employment, but only in favour of the employee. However, employees will be unable to rely on this provision in the context we are at present considering, since it only has application to exclusions in contracts made between employer and employee, not to those between employer and third party for the benefit of the employee. It is unlikely, however, that the reasonableness doctrine would upset a clause such as that in the *Satterthwaite* case, especially where it has been negotiated with such care and regard to detail, where adequate insurance has been undertaken, and where the various risks undertaken are reflected in the contract charges. There is ample evidence that the Privy Council felt the provision to be a reasonable one for commercial men to agree and it ought to be possible, at least in commercial agreements, to satisfy the statutory requirements without undue difficulty. In any event, by Schedule 1, section 2(2) does not apply to any contract of marine salvage or towage, any charterparty of a ship or hovercraft, and any contract for the carriage of goods by ship or hovercraft, except in favour of a person dealing as a consumer—an unlikely event in this field save in the case of contracts for personal carriage. In so far as contracts for the marine carriage of goods seem to have caused the law and the insurance world the most difficulty in this area it would seem that, aside from liability for death and personal injury, arrangements may proceed under the Act much as before. It is perhaps worth mentioning that section 3 of the Act, which prevents reliance on exclusion clauses by a party in breach of contract, will have no application where proceedings are brought directly against a third party whom the clause purports to protect. Section 3 is specifically limited to apply only "as between contracting parties," and then only when one of them deals as a consumer or on the other's standard terms of business.

Are there any other means, besides the use of complex clauses, whereby third parties can avoid the consequences of their negligence? There are several devices. One is for the third party to stipulate that the party with whom he is in privity must indemnify him, so that, for example, a consignor utilising the services of a forwarding agent for his goods may sue the carrier in tort or bailment in respect of the loss or damage to the goods. The carrier, in his contract with the forwarding agent, will require an indemnity for all claims losses and expenses, however arising.[25]

As we have seen in Chapter 1, section 4(1) of the 1977 Act applies the reasonableness doctrine to indemnity clauses imposed by a person in respect either of his own or his vacarious liability for negligence or breach of contract. This will be so where the obligation is to indemnify both the other party to the contract and/or a third party. However, the section only has application where the party upon whom the obligation to indemnify is imposed deals as a consumer, so the normal indemnity clauses found, for instance, in contracts between carriers and forwarding agents, all commercial men dealing by way of business, will be unaffected.

The second possibility is the argument of *volenti non fit injuria*. Lord Denning suggested in the *Midland Silicones* case[26] that if the stevedores had been mentioned in the bill of lading they might have been able to plead that the owners of goods, by signing it, consented to run the risk of negligence and were thus precluded from recovering in full when such negligence occurred. So far this possibility has the judicial support of Lord Denning alone, in a dissenting judgment at that. Both Beatty J. at first instance and Lord Simons in the Privy Council rejected it in *Satterthwaite*. It has the further difficulty that the *volenti* doctrine normally operates to exclude liability completely so that, whilst the argument may be viable where there is a clause protecting against any liability, it is difficult to see how it could apply to a case like *Satterthwaite* where the stevedores were claiming a limitation, but not a total exclusion, of liability. In any event, section 2(3) of the Unfair Contract Terms Act 1977 now provides that a person may not have a plea of *volenti non fit injuria* raised against him simply because he agreed to, or was aware of, a clause or notice which purports to exclude or restrict liability for negligence. Again, however, in the context in which this possibility has so far been canvassed, the Act has no impact since section 1(2) and Schedule 1 excludes the operation of section 2(3) in contracts of marine salvage or towage, in any charterparty of a ship or hovercraft, and in any contract for the carriage of goods by ship or hovercraft, save where one of the parties deals as a consumer.

Another possibility is the stay of action. This has been expressed by Treitel thus[27]: " ... an exemption clause in a contract between A and B may contain an express promise by A to B not to sue C. ... B can enforce that promise by getting a stay of any action by A against C, particularly if there is a contract between B and C under which B is bound to indemnify

C against liability incurred." This argument is based upon the decision of Ormrod J. in *Snelling* v. *John G. Snelling Ltd.*[28] In this case, three brothers had lent money to a family company of which they were directors, covenanting that if any of them resigned he should give up any rights to recover any money due to him from the company. One of them did resign and attempted to recover the amounts owing to him by the company. The company relied on the brother's covenant by way of defence and, since the company, as a separate legal entity, was not a party to the agreement, requested that the other two brothers be joined as defendants to the action. They duly were and counterclaimed for a declaration that, according to the terms of the plaintiff's agreement with them, the loan should be forfeited. They obtained the declaration, but Ormrod J. further held that they would obtain a stay of the action brought by the plaintiff against the defendant company. Ormrod J. decided that circuity of action must be avoided, *i.e.* it was undesirable that the plaintiff should be allowed to succeed against the defendant only to have himself sued for breach of his own agreement with the other two brothers, who would then recover from him the sum repaid by the company. To avoid this unnecessary litigation, Ormrod J. dismissed the action.

However, there are difficulties here. The amount the plaintiff could recover from the company was the amount of the loan. The amount the brothers could recover would be damages for breach of contract, which would arguably be nominal since they had lost nothing personally.[29] So, staying the action produces a different result from allowing all parties to sue out their respective claims. Translating this to the exclusion clause given by Treitel, it is arguable that B's claim against A is in contract, where again nominal damages will pertain, whereas A's claim against C will be in tort. This will not be so, however, if B is bound to indemnify C, so that C's loss becomes B's loss. In this case the stay of action argument ought to succeed, though the indemnity clause is an essential, rather than optional, element. It will be remembered that under section 4(1) of the 1977 Act some indemnity clauses may not, however, be upheld, and this seriously jeopardises the argument. Once this indemnity becomes essential, of course, the practical possibility of the stay of proceedings device actually being used recedes dramatically. The device depends upon two factors: first, the other party to the contract consenting to being joined as defendant, and secondly, the first defendant *requesting* the indemnifier to be joined. The certain knowledge that an indemdnity may be claimed should judgment go against the third party defendant is likely, in the view of the Road Haulage Association in any event, who use such an indemnity clause in their standard form conditions, to mitigate against any request for the third party to be joined in the proceedings. When one adds to that the possibility that, in some cases, the indemnity itself may not be upheld, then the practical possibility of the stay of proceedings being viable recedes even further.

B. *May a Third Party Incur the Burden of the Clause?*

It is less frequently the case, but none the less significant for that, that it is the party to the main contract who is claiming the benefit of the exclusion clause, and it is the third party against whom it is sought to exclude or limit rights.

In *Pyrene Co. Ltd.* v. *Scindia Navigation Co. Ltd.*[30] the sellers of a fire tender under an f.o.b. contract agreed that the buyers should make arrangements with the carrier for carriage. While the tender was being loaded it was damaged as a result of the carrier's negligence. Since the goods had not crossed the ship's rail when the damage occurred, they were still at the sellers' risk. The buyers and the carrier were parties to the bill of lading under which the carrier's liability was limited. The sellers claimed against the carrier for the damage

to the tender, and were met with the limditation provisions in
the bill of lading. Devlin J. first seemed to hold, without any
great confidence, that the seller might, for some purposes, be
treated as a party to the bill of lading.[31] It is difficult to see
how this can be so, since they are nowhere mentioned as
parties and it is inconsistent with the doctrine of privity.
However, Devlin J. proffered two further explanations which
are far more acceptable. He argued that the buyers were the
sellers' agent in making the contract of carriage, at least so far
as it concerned the sellers.[32] As a third possibility he
suggested that:

> "By delivering the goods alongside the seller impliedly
> invited the shipowner to load them, and the shipowner by
> lifting the goods impliedly accepted that invitation. The
> implied contract so created must incorporate the ship-
> owner's usual terms; none other would have been contem-
> plated; the shipowner would not contract for the loading of
> the goods on terms different from those which he offered
> for the voyage as a whole."[33]

This is perhaps the most satisfactory explanation of all. The
limitation of the carrier's liability was on the terms of
Art.IV(5) of the Hague Rules which, by the Carriage of
Goods by Sea Act 1924, were generally incorporated into all
such bills of lading. So, whilst no express mention of the limitation of liability had been made to the seller, he could be
taken to have known, as would all businessmen connected
with the export trade, that the carrier would handle cargo
only on those terms. By delivering the goods alongside the
seller made an implied invitation to the carrier to handle
them, and at the same time accepted the terms which the
carrier had, by implication, made a condition of his doing
so.

It would seem, therefore, that if an implied contract can be
raised along the lines of that inferred by Devlin J. in the

Pyrene case, then a third party can find himself carrying the burden of the clause. It will be recalled that a similar argument, based on an implied contract between the stevedores and the consignees, found favour with the Privy Council in the *Satterthwaite* case.[34].

Under the Unfair Contract Terms Act 1977, however, the third party will be able to make advantage of section 2(1) in respect of liability for negligence in just the same way as the contracting party can in the circumstances discussed earlier in this Chapter. The same will apply for section 2(2) and (3), subject to the qualifications already mentioned. If Devlin J.'s analysis in the *Pyrene* case is correct, and the third party's liability turns on the existence of an implied contract, then presumably *any* exclusion or limitation clause (not just one dealing with negligence) will be subject to the test of reasonableness, provided the third party deals as a consumer or the contract is in standard form, by virtue of section 3. As is explained in Chapter 6, section 3 applies the reasonableness test to exclusion clauses purporting to protect against breach when those clauses are raised by one party to the contract against the other. If the *Pyrene* case reasoning depends upon an implied contract, that implied contract will make the third party a party to the contract for the purpose of clause 3.

Notes

1 *Tweddle* v. *Atkinson* (1861) 1 B. & S. 393; *Dunlop Pneumatic Tyre Co. Ltd.* v. *Selfridge & Co. Ltd.* [1915] A.C.847; *Beswick* v. *Beswick* [1968] A.C.58; Furmston (1960) 23 M.L.R. 383-384; Finlay, *Third Party Contracts, passim.*

2 *Sykes* v. *Sykes* (1870) L.R. 5 C.P.113; *Hill* v. *Curtis* (1866) 35 L.J. Ch.133; *Anderson* v. *Watson* (1827) 3 C. & P. 214; *Stephens* v. *Elwall* (1815) 4 M. & S. 295.

3   [1924] A.C.522.
4   At p. 534.
5   See Treitel, *The Law of Contract* (4th ed.), p. 428.
6   Viscount Finlay at p. 534; Lord Sumner at pp. 564-565: Lord Dunedin agreed with the speech of Lord Sumner at p. 548, and Lord Carson agreed with both Lord Sumner and Viscount Cave at p. 565. See *Scruttons Ltd.* v. *Midland Silicones Ltd.* [1962] A.C.446, *per* Lord Denning at p. 487.
7   Coote, *Exception Clauses,* p. 132.
8   (1925) 21 Ll. L.R. 375 at p. 377.
9   *Per* Lord Denning in *Scruttons Ltd.* v. *Midland Silicones Ltd.* [1962] A.C.446 at p. 487.
10   *Cosgrove* v. *Horsefall* (1945) 62 T.L.R. 140; see also *Genys* v. *Matthews* [1966] 1 W.L.R. 758; *Gore* v. *Van der Lann* [1967] 2 Q.B.31; *Buckpitt* v. *Oates* [1968] 1 All E.R.1145; Odgers (1970) 86 L.Q.R. 69.
11   *Adler* v. *Dickson* [1955] 1 Q.B.158.
12   See Hanson [1959] C.L.J. 150; Coote, *Exception Clauses,* pp. 129-136.
13   [1962] A.C.446.
14   See *Adler* v. *Dickson* [1955] 1 Q.B.158.
15   *Ibid.*; *Gore* v. *Van der Lann* [1967] 2 Q.B.31.
16   Merchant Shipping Act 1956, s.3; Carriage by Air Act 1961, Sched. 1, art. 25A. Carriage of Goods by Sea Act 1971, Sched., art. IV.
17   Law of Property Act 1925, s.56.
18   [1975] A.C.154. See Reynolds (1974) 90 L.Q.R. 301; Coote (1974) 37 M.L.R. 453; Palmer [1974] J.B.L. 101, 220.
19   After the clause in *Adler* v. *Dickson* [1955] 1 Q.B.158.
20   [1972] N.Z.L.R. 385 (Beatty J.); [1973] 1 N.Z.L.R.174 (N.Z.C. of A.).
21   N.Z. Mercantile Law Act 1908, s.13.
22   *Brandt* v. *Liverpool, Brazil and River Plate Steam Navigation Co. Ltd.* [1924] 1 K.B.575; *cf. Margarine Union GmbH* v. *Cambay Prince Steamship Co. Ltd.* [1969] 1 Q.B.219; and see Reynolds (1974) 90 L.Q.R. 301 at p. 305.
23   At pp. 167-168.
24   At p. 168.
25   See *Lee Cooper & Co. Ltd.* v. *C. H. Jeakins Ltd.* [1967] 2 Q.B.1; *Gillespie Bros. Ltd.* v. *Roy Bowles Transport Ltd.* [1973] 1 Q.B.400; and see Road Haulage Association's Conditions of Carriage.
26   [1962] A.C.446 at p. 488.
27   *Law of Contract* (4th ed.), p. 430.
28   [1973] 1 Q.B.87.
29   *Beswick* v. *Beswick* [1968] A.C.58.
30   [1954] 2 Q.B.402.
31   At p. 426.

32 At pp. 423-425.
33 At p. 426.
34 [1975] A.C.154 at pp. 167-168, although the New Zealand courts preferred to rely on statutory provisions.

Chapter 6

BREACH OF FUNDAMENTAL TERM AND FUNDAMENTAL BREACH

Even if an exclusion clause forms a part of the contract, a party seeking to rely on it will have to overcome three more hurdles. First, he may have to rebut evidence that he has not performed his contract in its essential respects, *i.e.* that he has committed a breach of a fundamental term of the contract. Secondly, he will have to show that, notwithstanding the absence of any such breach, the exemption clause can be construed, without ambiguity, to cover the consequences of the particular breach of contract which has occurred. Thirdly, he may have to be prepared to justify the exclusion clause as "reasonable" according to certain statutory tests. A very great deal of effort, both academic[1] and judicial, has been devoted to finding a rational basis for these apparently simple paths to success in litigation on a contract containing an exemption clause. The result is a veritable maze of blind alleys and confusion. The law in this area is uncertain and unnecessarily complex, largely as a result of litigation over the last 20 years coupled with hasty legislative activity. In the next chapter it is proposed to consider how some of this complexity can be removed from the law. This chapter is concerned with explaining the substance and evolution of this complexity. It is submitted that it is only with reference to the historical development of two doctrines that the present law can be understood.

There is arguably authority for the proposition that in every contract there are certain obligations, sometimes express but more usually implied, which are fundamental, the breach of which amounts to a complete non-performance of the contract. These terms differ from normal contractual conditions in at least one important respect; their presence is essential to the very core and essence of the contract and liability in the event of breach cannot be excluded by means of exemption clauses, since to do so would deprive the agreement of its contractual content. Closely connected with this principle is the doctrine of fundamental breach. A person commits such a breach by breaking a term of a contract other than a "fundamental" term in a manner that has consequences for the injured party that are far more disastrous, or "fundamental," than would be the case for a mere breach of condition.

A. *Breach of a Fundamental Term: A Definition*

Whether or not there has been a breach of a fundamental term depends upon whether the promisor has performed the obligation which forms the essential character and base of the contract. The most famous example, and one which is now of some antiquity, is that of Lord Abinger in *Chanter* v. *Hopkins*[2] who observed " ... If a man offers to buy peas of another, and he sends him beans, he does not perform his contract, ... the contract is to sell peas, and if he sends him anything else in their stead, it is a non-performance of it." More recently the same idea was expressed by Devlin J. in *Smeaton Hanscomb* v. *Sassoon I Setty*.[3] In that case the plaintiffs had contracted to purchase a quantity of mahogany logs, in process of shipment from Lagos to Liverpool, from the defendants. They were to be of "fair quality" and of specified dimensions but "should any dispute arise ... the buyers shall nevertheless accept the goods ... and make due payment ... such payment, however, shall not affect their right, if any, to claim compensation for breach of contract. Such difference shall be referred to arbitration and ... any claim must be made within 14 days of final discharge of the goods.'' Final discharge was completed at Liverpool on June 6, 1951. Five weeks later the plaintiffs complained both of the quality and of the dimensions and claimed to reject the logs. The defendants set up the clause quoted but the plaintiffs argued that the clause should not apply because the sellers had broken a fundamental term of the contract. The theoretical merits of such an argument will be examined later, but Devlin J. held that the clause protected the defendants. There had, on the facts, been no breach of a fundamental term. Devlin J., in the course of his judgment, propounded a definition of a fundamental term[4]: ''Something which underlies the whole contract, so that if it is not complied with the performance becomes totally different from that which the contract contemplates.'' So, the breach of a fundamental term, then, results in performance so ''totally different'' that there can be, in effect, no performance at all of the actual obligation agreed under the contract. If there are any goods or services proffered they are so different from those stipulated that they are not referrable to the fundamental obligation undertaken by the contract.

Further examples can be taken from the law relating to the sale of goods. As we have seen, section 12(1)(*a*) of the Sale of Goods Act 1893 implies into every contract for the sale of goods, other than one to which subsection (2) applies, certain undertakings as to title. Section 1(1) of the same Act defines a contract for the sale of goods as a contract ''whereby the seller transfers or agrees to transfer the property in the goods to the buyer.'' It has been suggested[5] that a seller who cannot transfer such property cannot perform the fundamental obligation of a contract for the sale of goods and therefore that a breach of section 12(1)(*a*) of the Sale of Goods Act

1893 must, of necessity, involve the seller in a breach of a fundamental term of the contract.[6] This proposition received tacit support in the decision of the Court of Appeal in *Rowland* v. *Divall*.[7] The plaintiff contracted to buy a motor vehicle from the defendant. The car was delivered to him and he used it for four months. It then appeared that it was the property of a third party. The plaintiff surrendered it to its rightful owner and sued the defendant to recover the price. The Court of Appeal held that there had been a total failure of the consideration contracted for and that the plaintiff was thus entitled to recover the full purchase price paid.[8] A person who purports to sell goods which are not his to sell will not have performed the contract in its essential respects (unless s.12(2) of the 1893 Act has been incorporated into the contract instead of s.12(1)) and will therefore commit a breach of a fundamental term of the contract.

The same principle can be applied to the case of goods sold by description. Section 13(1) of the Sale of Goods Act 1893 prescribes that: "Where there is a contract for the sale of goods by description, there is an implied condition that the goods shall correspond with that description." However, such an implied term would seem to be an additional undertaking, given by the seller who sells goods by description, to some fundamental term of similar character, since excluding it (where this is possible) does not seem to affect the rights of a buyer to repudiate the contract where the goods supplied do not correspond with the description.[9] A failure to supply goods corresponding with the contract description might, therefore, amount to a breach of a fundamental term of the contract.[10] This would, however, only be so where the failure of the goods to correspond with the description resulted in goods being supplied of a totally different kind from those contracted for, since only then would there be a failure of consideration.[11] In *Pinnock Bros.* v. *Lewis & Peat*[12] the plaintiff agreed to purchase 100 bags of copra cake to be used as cattle food. The copra cake contained such a high proportion of castor beans as to render it dangerous to cattle. Roche J. said[13]: " ... I hold that the delivery in this case could not be properly described as copra cake at all." The plaintiffs had delivered a substance quite different from that contracted for. They had not performed their contract in a fundamental respect and the breach of this fundamental term resulted in their failing to supply the consideration contracted for.

There are clearly problems with this approach and it has been trenchantly criticised.[14] How does one define the *genus* contracted for? What if the vendor attempts to reserve himself latitude by incorporating a clause conferring an option to vary the description (although arguably this would be caught by the Unfair Contract Terms Act 1977).[15] What degree of seriousness can be tolerated in defects before the *genus* becomes different? What is the relationship between the fundamental term of the contract and the description attached to the subject matter? A failure to comply with the contract description can surely be a breach of an express term of the contract, implied terms and fundamental terms notwithstanding. Despite these problems the courts have consistently applied the "difference in kind" reasoning, even in cases where a very modest outlay would restore the article to the contract *genus*[16] and there is a substantial body of authority to the effect that a breach of a fundamental term amounts to a total failure of consideration. In that event, the courts have held, an exclusion clause, for the reasons explained below, will not, at common law, apply, although in regard to those cases falling within the Unfair Contract Terms Act 1977, the position is, as we shall see, different.

B. *When Does Consideration Totally Fail?*

The word "consideration" appears to have two totally

different meanings in the law of contract. In one sense it is the benefit conferred by the promisee, or the detriment incurred by the promisor as the "price" of the promise without which the promise is gratuitous and, unless under seal, will be unenforceable. If the consideration fails in this sense, the promisor's promise will turn out to be void or illusory.[17] The other context in which the term is used is in relation to performance. It is in this sense that the word is used in the context of breach of a fundamental term. A total failure of consideration is a failure to perform the contract in its essential respects. In this sense it can operate to found an action in quasi-contract for money had and received,[18] to indicate a defence to actions in contract,[19] to permit the terms of a contract to be ignored so as to allow another cause of action, *e.g.* bailment,[20] or, in the absence of an operative exclusion clause, to found an action in damages for breach.

In each of these situations total failure of consideration has the same meaning in the sense that it means non-performance. However, where it denotes a defence, unless the contract is severable,[21] failure of consideration may have the result that the promisee is under no obligation to make any payment in respect of an uncompleted contract[22] whilst not being able to sue for breach or to recover in quasi-contract anything he might have already paid. So, what would be a failure of consideration sufficient to relieve the promisee from further obligations might well not be a "total" failure for the purpose of the quasi-contractual remedy.[23] The two situations turn on different degrees of performance, or, put another way, whether the obligation broken is fundamental.

In *Fibrosa Spolka Akeyjna* v. *Fairburn Lawson Combe Barbour Ltd.*[24] Viscount Simon L.C. said: "When one is considering the law of failure of consideration ... it is generally speaking, not the promise which is referred to as the consideration, but the performance of the promise." So, the test is whether one party, in performance of the contract, has conferred any benefit on the other: it is not a matter of whether that other has received *any* benefit, but whether he has received any part of the particular benefit which he was entitled to expect by way of performance of the contract. Failure of consideration may still be total even though the defendant has incurred detriment in attempting to perform his part of the contract.[25] For there to be no total failure, the promisee must actually receive part of what he contracted to receive,[26] or for some reason, such as wrongfully refusing to accept the promisor's tender, be disentitled to allege otherwise.[27] Total failure of consideration in no way depends upon the fault of the defendant. Where it occurs through the fault of one party, it will be a breach of a fundamental term; where it occurs without fault, it may still be a breach of a fundamental term where one party has assumed the risk of impossibility of performance,[28] otherwise it will be frustration.[29]

C. *The Effect of Breach of a Fundamental Term on Exclusion Clauses*

The significance of this discussion on total failure of consideration is that the courts have held that where a party commits a breach of a fundamental term he will not be able to rely on any clause of exemption or limitation in order to enforce the contract against the other party. Statutory provisions have made inroads into this principle and these will be discussed later, but at common law the effect of a breach of a fundamental term was to deprive the exclusion clause of any effect. So, in *Pinnock Bros.* v. *Lewis & Peat Ltd.*[30] the contract contained a clause which stated that "goods are not warranted free from defects rendering the same unmerchantable, which would not be apparent on reasonable examination, any statute or rule of law notwithstanding." Roche J. held that: "Where a substance quite different from that contracted for has been delivered, that clause has no application." There are many other cases in which this principle has been applied.[31]

In *Yeoman Credit Ltd.* v. *Apps*[32] a hirer hired a car under a contract of hire-purchase that, contrary to his expectations, had such an accumulation of defects on delivery, not being apparent defects, as to make it unusable. The contract contained an exclusion clause. Holroyd Pearce L.J. said[33]:

> "Whether there has been a breach of a fundamental condition of the agreement is a question of degree depending on the facts. Such a breach is different in weight and gravity from breaches of condition which would come within the exemption. It may be ... an accumulation of defects which, taken singly, might well have been within the exemption clause, but taken en masse constitute such a non-performance or repudiation or breach going to the root of the contract as disentitles the owners to take refuge behind an exception clause intended only to give protection to those breaches which are not inconsistent with and not destructive of the whole essence of the contract."

Harman L.J. said, in the same case[34]: "It has always been held, as I understand it, that an exception clause cannot be used to avoid what, in the case of chattels, seems to be a fundamental condition." Discussing contracts for reality, he says: " ... it has always been the doctrine among real property lawyers that such a clause [*i.e.* an exemption clause] though apparently covering the event, never protected the vendor if the misdescription were of so grave a character as altogether to alter the bargain made, going, ... to the root of the bargain." Harman L.J. clearly has in mind here the rule known as the rule in *Flight* v. *Booth,*[35] a rule of common law origin to the effect that a vendor will be unable to enforce a contract for the sale of land, either at law or in equity, even with an abatement of the price, where there has been a substantial misdescription. This will be so even where there is a clause in the contract to the effect that no misdescriptions shall annul the sale.[36] The rationale of the rule was expressed by Eve J. in *Lee* v. *Rayson*,[37] where he makes it plain that what the property lawyers have in mind is not simply a question of whether the purchaser is to get value for money, but something much closer to the commercial lawyer's notion of breach of a fundamental term:

> "A vendor could not fulfil a contract to sell Whiteacre by conveying Blackacre, although he might prove to demonstration that the value of the latter was largely in excess of the value of the former. Value, no doubt, is an element to be taken into account in determining whether an error in description is substantial or material, but it is certainly not the only element, nor, in my opinion, the dominant one."

To return to Harman L.J., he, by arguing by analogy with contracts for the disposition of interests in real property, apparently endorses the view that supplying something totally different from the consideration contracted for destroys the protection of the exclusion clause. It would seem that this is because the contract can in that event be terminated. Should this be so and why should termination of the contract be significant?

The cases so far cited are some evidence for a general common law principle to the effect that where there has been a breach of a fundamental term, and by this is meant a failure of consideration, the contract cannot be enforced against the innocent party by the party in breach, (although this will be affected by the Unfair Contract Terms Act 1977[38], the presence of an exclusion or limitation clause notwithstanding. Looking at the situation from the point of view of the innocent party who is faced with a breach of a fundamental term, what action can he take? The answer can perhaps best be found by examination of a particular example, for instance a non-consumer[39] contract for the sale of goods by description. There will be a total failure of consideration if the goods delivered to the buyer are so defective that they cannot properly be described as the goods promised under the contract at all; so take an example already considered, copra cake very heavily adulterated with castor beans. The buyer's remedy here is obviously to reject the goods. If he decides instead to accept them, then he makes a new contract. The reason for this is that if there has been such a serious breach of section 13(1) of the Sale of Goods Act 1893 as to amount to a total failure of consideration, the goods proffered cannot in any sense be referrable to the contract which must, *ipso facto*, be regarded as terminated. There can be nothing of the consideration contracted for in that contract to accept. There is, therefore, an *automatic* repudiation in the event of a breach of a fundamental term.[40] That being so, acceptance of such defective goods as are proferred will amount to acceptance of a new and entirely separate offer,[41] and the courts will not necessarily imply into this new contract an exclusion clause that was present in the old one. The right to damages for breach of the first contract, however, will survive (disregarding, for the moment, any problems with the exclusion clause) because the promisee's rights under that contract have not been surrendered. The defendant provides no consideration for any implied undertaking that may be given to release him from liability for his breach.

When the innocent party repudiates for breach of a fundamental term (as he needs must do), there is some dispute as to whether the repudiation operates from the date when the election to repudiate is made or from the date of the breach.[42] However, whichever view is preferred, it is clear that until such time as it is repudiated, the contract remains valid and binding and all its terms, including the exclusion clause, continue to operate as agreed between the parties. As one commentator convincingly argues,[43] the buyer's right to repudiate and his right of action to damages would accrue at a time when the exclusion clause, along with all the other terms of the contract, is still on foot and his success or failure would be governed by that clause. But, as we have seen, the authorities seem to permit the victim of a total failure of consideration to ignore the exclusion clause. The solution lies in the fact that there is not just one group of cases here, but three. First there are those cases in which the plaintiff is simply seeking the return of money already paid. Secondly is a group of cases in which damages are recovered, but on some other ground, and thirdly is a very small group of cases where damages have been awarded on the contract.

If we return to our example based upon a contract for the sale of goods, a buyer faced with a breach of a fundamental term but who has already paid for the goods, can repudiate the contract by rejecting such purported performance as the seller offers. To recover the purchase price he does not need to rely on the contract for an action in damages, and hence he need not be concerned with the exclusion clause. This is a necessary result of treating the exclusion clause simply as a shield against damages claims, rather than as modifying the obligation-defining terms of the contract. The buyer can recover any money paid by a quasi-contractual action for money had and received. Although such a proposition is not entirely free from doubt, there are at least two reasons why it can be supported.

First, section 54 of the Sale of Goods Act 1893 seems to regard an action for the price paid as being a separate issue from that of damages: "Nothing in this Act shall affect the right of the buyer or the seller to recover interest or special damages in any case where by law interest or special damages may be recoverable, or to recover money paid where the consideration for the payment of it has failed."

Secondly, there are clear dicta to the effect that the remedy available to the innocent party who rejects for total failure of consideration, and who wishes to recover money paid, is quasi-contractual. Viscount Simon L.C. said in the *Fibrosa* case[44]:

"The claim of a party who has paid money under a contract to get the money back, on the ground that the consideration for which he paid it has totally failed, is not based upon any provision contained in the contract, but arises because, in the circumstances which have happened, the law gives a remedy in quasi contract to the party who has not got that for which he bargained. It is a claim to recover money to which the defendant has no further right because, in the circumstances, which have happened, the money must be regarded as received to the plaintiff's use."

One consequence of this, of course, is that whilst the victim of a breach of a fundamental term can recover any money he has paid over to the party in breach, despite the presence of an exclusion clause, he cannot recover by way of compensation *in contract* damages for any other property handed over *e.g.* pursuant to a contract of carriage, nor can he recover for consequential loss. This is because at the time when the loss occurred, which was the time of the breach, the contract, including the exclusion clause, was still in force. Logically, therefore, the exclusion clause ought to protect the "guilty" party unless it can, on its construction, be held not to cover the events that have occurred.[45] However, there are some authorities that would seem to contradict this proposition to the extent that damages have been awarded to the victim of a breach of fundamental term where a close construction of the exclusion clause did not seem to be a factor uppermost in the court's mind. The key to these cases lies in the fact that firstly, they are nearly all bailments, and secondly, an alternative remedy was in every case available to an action on the contract itself.

A bailee of goods incurs under the general law certain obligations dependent upon his status, and quite independent of his liability in contract. The obligations of the bailee are founded on negligence. He is under a duty to take care of the goods bailed and whilst the degree of care may vary slightly with the type of bailment[46] it is a duty which at common law exists quite apart from any contract and which is imposed on the bailee because he has been put in possession of another's goods. A consequence of this is that the owner of goods may succeed against the bailee with an action for damages by reason of the loss or damage to the goods, although in the circumstances of the case there is no contract. So, if A hands goods to a carrier for carriage and delivery, it is only A who makes any contract with the carrier, but if the goods are actually the property of B, possibly because B has already bought them from A or because A, who has possession of the goods, is B's employee,[47] not only A, the contracting party, but also B, a third party, may claim damages from the carrier if the goods are lost or damaged. If A is a forwarding agent who entrusts B's property to a carrier, A normally acts as consignor and party to the contract of carriage, but B can nevertheless claim damages against the carrier if the goods are lost or damaged.[48]

In most cases a bailee is not liable for loss or injury to the goods while in his charge, unless the loss or injury was due to his wilful act or negligence. The ordinary bailee is only bound to take reasonable care of the other person's goods. If the goods are lost or destroyed without any negligence on his part, he is under no liability, but the burden is on him to prove that the damage was not due to his negligence, and if he fails in such proof he is held responsible.[49]

All bailees are subject to fault liability, but common carriers (and this includes carriers by sea) and innkeepers are, by virtue of their common calling, subjected to a further liability quite independent of fault.[50] This is a strict liability[51] under which the bailee incurs a strict responsibility in respect of any loss, destruction or damage to the goods bailed,[52] the only defences he may set up being act of God, act of the Queen's enemies, inherent vice in the bailed goods, and wrongful act of the bailor.

The ordinary bailee, therefore, is subject to two tiers of liability: his liability in contract and his status liability based on fault. The common carrier is subject to three tiers of liability, that under contract, that for negligence, and his strict liability for loss, destruction or damage to the bailed goods. Under the common law[53] both the status liability and the strict liability could be modified by contract, usually by appropriately worded exclusion clauses, and these will protect the bailee whilst the contract is still on foot. But, if the contract is automatically repudiated for total failure of consideration, such as occurs in the case of breach of a fundamental term, there is no need to rely on that contract to recover damages for any loss sustained. As a matter of fact and law the bailment would still have existed at the time of loss or damage to the goods, and whilst the bailor may not be able to recover damages on the contract, he will be able to recover on the basis of the bailee's status or strict liability.

This appears to be the thinking underlying the early cases on breach of a fundamental term which have their origin not in sale of goods and hire-purchase, but in contracts of carriage. However, there is one fundamental misconception that must be avoided and that is that where there is concurrent liability in contract and some other ground, such as bailment or tort, and the contract is repudiated, it leaves the other liability intact as if there had never been a contract in the first place. Such a view presupposes that when a carrier is disqualified from relying on an exemption clause by reason of breach of a fundamental term, the liability which the exemption originally excluded somehow survives the exclusion and is revived by the carrier's wrongful act.[54] This is not so. If, for example, a common carrier excludes his strict liability by contract, he remains exempted throughout the duration of the contract from this strict liability. If loss or damage occurs, it must be whilst the contract is still on foot, since repudiation does not occur until after the event causing such loss or damage, and consequently it must be whilst the protection against liability is still operative. When the carrier's fault results in damage for which he is held liable, this depends not on a revived strict liability, but on his liability for fault *qua* bailee. It must follow from this, therefore, that in those cases in which damages are nevertheless awarded, it is because the exclusion clause has not been construed to exclude every liability, *i.e.* in contract, for fault and, in the case of the common carrier, his strict liability.

The argument only occurs in a very small class of case, simply because it is extremely difficult for a bailee to do anything in relation to the goods, short of deliberately destroying them, that amounts to a total failure of consideration for the contract of bailment. Such non-performance may, however, arise where the bailee contracts to store goods in warehouse A and in fact stores them in warehouse B where they are damaged.[55] The so-called "four-corners" rule discussed in Chapter 4[56] can be seen as a further application of the total failure of consideration principle, permitting repudiation of the contract and the award of damages on the basis of some concurrent liability. A bailee who steps outside the "four corners" of the contract cannot, whatever else he may be doing, be regarded as performing the contract he has promised to perform. His performance, once he steps outside the "four corners," is not referrable to his agreement. His agreement, therefore, remains unperformed and this, as has been argued above, amounts to a breach of a fundamental term. The bailor may often claim compensation, not on the contract but on the bailment.

So, in *London & North Western Railway* v. *Neilson,*[57]

theatrical properties were consigned by rail from Llandudno to Bolton via Manchester. They were placed by the railway company in a special van and labels were affixed to the van indicating its destination. These labels came off en route. As a result, the van was unloaded at Manchester and some of the properties were put in the station cloakroom, whilst others were returned to wherever the old labels on their cases indicated. A clause in the contract of carriage exempted the railway company from liability for loss, damage, misconveyance, misdelivery, delay or detention of the goods. The House of Lords held that, when the goods were dispersed at Manchester, the company put an end to the agreed transit. It could not, therefore, rely on the exclusion clause. Lord Atkinson said[58]:

> "As soon as the carrier deliberately deviates from the stipulated route, he carries the goods where the consignor never agreed that they should be carried, and where he (the carrier) by his special contract never agreed that he would carry them. So far from performing the duty to which the special protective provision applies, he abandons the attempt to perform it — ceases to act in accordance with it, in fact violates it."

In *Joseph Thorley Ltd.* v. *Orchis Steamship Co. Ltd.*[59] a cargo of beans was shipped by the defendants' boat from Limassol to London. The bill of lading exempted the defendants from liability arising from any act, neglect or default of themselves or their agents in loading, stowing or discharging the cargo. The ship deviated from her agreed route during the voyage. While the beans were being discharged in London, they were damaged by contamination. The defendants pleaded the exclusion clause. It was held that it was unnecessary to connect the loss which had occured to the deviation. By deviating the defendants had voluntarily substituted another voyage for that stipulated in the bill of lading. The plaintiffs could not accept that substituted voyage without, by definition, accepting a new contract. Hence the original contract was automatically terminated as a result of the total failure of consideration and so the defendants could not claim the benefit of the exclusion clause when sued as bailees outside the contract. Fletcher Moulton L.J. said[60] that a shipowner guilty of a deviation cannot be considered as having performed his part of a bill of lading contract but something "fundamentally different."

Whether or not the bailee is acting totally outside his contract will depend, of course, on what he has promised to do. A bailee who deliberately destroys the goods entrusted to his care clearly fails to provide the consideration contracted for by the bailor notwithstanding the presence in the contract of a clause exempting the bailee from liability for loss or damage to the bailed goods. However, the question of performance depends on contractual intention and two approaches are, as we have seen, used to ascertain this. One is to examine the contract, apart from the clause, to ascertain what the parties intended. The other is to regard the contract as a series of promises defined both positively in the form of express or implied terms, or negatively in the form of exclusion clauses. On this latter view, in order to decide whether or not the bailee has provided any of the consideration contracted for, it is necessary to construe the exclusion clause in the same fashion as the other clauses are construed. It will be apparent that the former approach is more likely to result in a finding that the defendant's actions or non-actions amount to a total failure of the consideration contracted for, than is the latter approach. It has been suggested[61] that cases of bailment, and especially deviation cases, create peculiar problems and, for this reason, should be treated as a class apart, laying down no principles of general application. There seems no reason why such special pleading is necessary. These cases are simply further examples of situations in which the bailee may fail to provide the consideration contracted for (in which case, notwithstanding termination of the contract, he remains liable in bailment) or may not (in which case his liabilities remain governed by the contract).

Whether or not deviation constitutes a breach of a fundamental term depends, then, upon whether it constitutes nonperformance, which in turn depends upon the intention of the parties. The starting point will be an assumption that the parties did not intend the bailee to be protected on a journey not contemplated by the contract. This assumption derives from considerations of policy adopted by the judges in the last century.[62] The consignor was only able to secure insurance cover for his goods as long as they were in transit on the agreed route. Once the carrier deviated, the insurance cover ceased. If it were possible for the carrier successfully to exclude his status and contracted liability by means of an exemption clause, the owner of the goods would be unable to cover himself against any loss or damage occurring after deviation had taken place — a manifestly unhappy state of affairs. Hence, to protect the commercial interest thus threatened, the assumption in the earlier cases that deviation amounted to non-performance.[63] The courts could thus take advantage of an automatic termination of the contract that such a finding made possible, instead of putting the consignor to an election which, if not made in time, would have resulted in an inability to repudiate the contract. The bailor was thus enabled to recover his losses from the bailee, not in contract, but by virtue of the bailee's breach of duty. When insurers began to allow goods to be held covered during a deviation on payment of an extra premium, so that the bailor could recoup his losses from his insurers should he be unable to do so against the carrier, the courts started looking far more carefully at what would constitute non-performance under the contract, and this inevitably meant adopting a more careful construction of the terms of the contract, including the exclusion clause. It was this shift of emphasis on the importance of a close construction of the contract that resulted in many later deviations ceasing to be regarded as non-performance.[64] Indeed, the contract may then be construed as conferring on the carrier, by reason of exclusion, a liberty to deviate,[65] rather than being construed as a contract stipulating a fixed route with a clause granting relief from liability in damages if deviation occurs.

In the same way, although it will be a duty of a carrier to carry goods expeditiously to their destination, the question whether delay is covered by an exemption clause or whether it is regarded as going to the root of the contract will depend upon how the obligation-defining terms are construed.[66] Delay may be sufficient to amount to a total failure of consideration where the parties cannot be taken to have intended the exclusion clause to relieve the obligation to perform for the period of the delay,[67] or to alleviate a risk consequent upon the delay which is wholly at variance with the contract of carriage.[68] So, for example, where a person hired a van and driver for two and a half hours for the purpose of delivering goods to his customers expeditiously, and the goods were stolen when the driver left the van for an hour for lunch, it was held that this delay, not being within the contemplation of the contract, went to the root of the consideration, so that the carrier was not protected by a clause excluding liability for loss of the goods, and was liable on his bailment.[69] Similarly, in *Gibaud* v. *Great Eastern Railway*,[70] the plaintiff left his bicycle at the defendants' station and received a ticket containing a clause purporting to exempt the defendants from liability. The bicycle was not put in the cloakroom but left in the booking-hall, where it was stolen. The Court of Appeal held that if the contract had been to keep the bicycle necessarily in the cloakroom, the defendants would have stepped outside the "four corners" of the contract and not been protected by the exemption clause, which would only protect them whilst performing their contractual obligations, not their obligations as bailees.

The principle was summed up by Lord Hodson in *Suisse Atlantique Société d'Armement Maritine S.A.* v. *Rotterdamsche Kolen Centrale*[71]:

> "Under a contract of carriage or bailment if the carrier or bailee uses a place other than that agreed on for storing the goods, or otherwise exposes the goods to risks quite different from those contemplated by the contract, he cannot rely on clauses in the contract designed to protect him against liability within the four corners of the contract, and has only such protection as is afforded by the common law."

In the same way, unauthorised sub-contracting will also lie outside the four corners of the contract of bailment. A bailee who sub-contracts will, therefore, not be performing his contractual obligation at all, although he will remain liable as an ordinary bailee of the goods. In *Davies* v. *Collins*[72] an army officer sent his uniform to the defendant to be cleaned. It was accepted on the following conditions: "Whilst every care is exercised in cleaning and dyeing garments, all orders are accepted at owner's risk entirely and we are unable to hold ourselves responsible for damage ... liability for loss is limited to an amount not exceeding ten times the cost of cleaning." The uniform was never returned and it was shown that the defendant had sub-contracted the job of cleaning and this was how the loss occurred. The Court of Appeal held that the contract was one to be personally performed by the defendant and that the farming-out to a sub-contractor was outside the scope of the contract altogether. The defendant was therefore liable for the loss.

D. *Breach of Fundamental Term and the Unfair Contract Terms Act 1977*

Total failure of consideration, and hence breach of a fundamental term, is far more difficult to establish than it was as a result of the changes in approach adopted by the courts to the construction of the contractual terms. However, under the provision of the Unfair Contract Terms Act 1977 such unfashionable jurisprudence is made even less attractive. The success of the breach of fundamental term argument depended upon two factors. First, it depends upon the automatic termination of the contract as a result of the breach, and secondly, the availability of alternative remedies, in quasi contract, tort or bailment, that were not trammelled by the exclusion clause. Section 2(2) of the Unfair Contract Terms Act provides that in the case of loss or damage (other than death or personal injury, liability for which cannot be excluded at all) caused as a result of negligence, any exclusion clause or notice will only be effective if it satisfies the requirement of reasonableness already mentioned in Chapter 3. Negligence in this context is defined by section 1 as including both a duty imposed by contract and one imposed by the common law to take reasonable care or to exercise reasonable skill. By virtue of section 1(1)(*b*), however, it does not include any stricter common law duty, nor, by section 1(3), is it to apply other than to things done in the course of a business. So, it would cover a bailee's contractual and status liability for fault but not, it seems, the common carrier's strict liability. By Schedule 1, para. 2, the restrictions of section 2(2) in the cases of charterparties of ships or hovercraft, or contracts for the carriage of goods by ships or hovercraft, only apply where the person dealing with the carrier deals as a consumer.[73] Finally, section 9(1) provides that neither the termination of the contract in consequence of breach, nor as a result of a party electing to treat it as repudiated, will automatically invalidate an exemption clause which would otherwise be subject to the test of reasonableness under the Act.

So, returning then to our bailment cases, it would seem that the mere fact that there has been a breach of a fundamental term will not mean that an exclusion clause will automatically not apply (s. 9(1)). It will only be of no effect, when construed to apply to negligence, where it is held to be unreasonable, except that the reasonableness test does not apply to clauses purporting to exclude the common carrier's strict liability. In this case, section 9(1) does not apply either, and so where the concurrent liability of the bailee is strict as a common carrier, the old common law rules explained above will presumably still apply so far as that strict liability is concerned. So, there are now several possibilities. If the contract is a charterparty of a ship or hovercraft, or a contract for the carriage of goods by ship or hovercraft, and neither of the parties deals as a consumer, then the old common law rules apply. Where one of the parties does deal as a consumer, or the contract is of some other kind involving the exercise of reasonable care or skill, as in bailment, and the clause is construed so as to protect against negligence, then the exclusion clause cannot be automatically disregarded because of termination, even for breach of a fundamental term. Instead the court must first consider whether it is reasonable to allow reliance on the clause.[74] The burden of proving reasonableness is on the *proferens* (s. 11(5)). If the bailee is a common carrier, and the exclusion clause is construed as only covering the contractual liability and status liability for fault, the effect of a breach of a fundamental term would still be to operate an automatic termination of the contract under the common law; because the criterion of reasonableness has no application, section 9(1) has no application and the bailor can recover damages for breach of the bailee's strict duty.

The Act would seem to have no application either to claims for repayment of monies in the event of a breach of a fundamental term. Where the action is for money had and received on the ground that the consideration has totally failed, the quasi-contractual claim is not founded on the contract at all and so, *ipso facto,* the exclusion clause cannot apply and it is difficult to see how any provision in the Act can affect this.

It will be recalled that there was a third group of cases where there was no quasi-contractual claim, nor was there any concurrent liability and yet the court was prepared to allow an action for damages to succeed. There are only two possible grounds for such a decision. One is that the exclusion clause, on its construction, was not worded in such a way as to cover a breach of a fundamental term, and the other is that the judges misinterpreted, either by accident or design, the earlier decisions, failing to recognise that the award of damages depended upon the existence of some concurrent liability. It was this problem that led to the development of a closely related doctrine, that of fundamental breach.

E. *Fundamental Breach: A Definition*

A difficulty created by the tendency of the courts, commented on in section C above, to take a more rigorous approach to the construction of contractual terms in general and exclusion clauses in particular, consequent upon the increasing availability of excepted loss insurance cover, was that certain breaches of contract could not, or could no longer, be regarded as going to the root of the consideration contracted for. Further, whilst treating a breach of contract as a breach of a fundamental term suited a contracting party who simply wished to repudiate the contract and claim repayment of monies or to resist enforcement of the contract against him, it did not assist the party who wished to pursue a remedy in damages, unless he could fall back upon some concurrent liability such as tort or bailment. Once exclusion clauses became common in contracts for the sale of goods and hire-purchase, there was a real difficulty for the buyer or hirer who, even if he successfully repudiated the contract for breach of a fundamental term, ought not, in strict law, to be able to make the seller or owner liable in damages for breach. This is because in many cases the exclusion clause clearly protected the *proferens* against liability in contract and in these cases that was the only liability. There was, in most sales and hire-purchase contracts, no surviving liability for breach of the duty of care.

These two problems made it necessary to find some other means to enable the innocent party to circumvent the oppressive operation of certain clauses of exclusion and limitation and this in turn gave rise to the development of the doctrine of fundamental breach. Added impetus was given to the search for a new legal solution to the problems of exclusion clauses by the emergence, at about the same time, of a certain degree of concern for the protection of the "consumer interest," and a feeling that perhaps too much concern had been shown in the past towards the preservation of an outmoded ideal of freedom of contract and the furtherance of the "commercial interest." The doctrine of breach of a fundamental term is concerned with performance of contractual obligations. If the promisor, by not performing at all or by proferring performance that cannot be made referrable to his promises under the contract, fails to provide the consideration contracted for, then he commits a breach of a fundamental term. But what if he does perform his contract; what if he acts within the "four corners" of the contract, but does so in such a deficient manner that very serious consequences ensue for the promissee? Then he commits a fundamental breach of contract. So, a fundamental breach is a breach of a contractual obligation. It is not one that goes to the root of the consideration, but nevertheless has disastrous consequences in terms of loss for the other party. So here, then, the law is concerned not with the fundamental nature of the obligation broken, but with the consequences of that breach. This distinction was put by Megaw L.J. in the case of *Wathes (Western) Ltd.* v. *Austins (Menswear) Ltd.*[75]:

> "The distinction between the breach of a fundamental term and a fundamental breach of a term which is not itself fundamental is now well recognized. Viscount Dilhorne, in *Suisse Atlantique Société d'Armement Maritine S.A.* v. *N.V. Rotterdamsche Kolen Centrale* [1967] A.C. 361 at p. 541 put it thus: 'Although the terms are sometimes used as if their meaning was the same, a fundamental breach differs from a breach of a fundamental term' ... Perhaps the words [used by the judge at first instance] indicate a failure to distinguish fully between a breach of a fundamental term and a fundamental breach. If it were a question of a breach of a fundamental term, events consequent upon the breach might be irrelevant. But to justify a finding of fundamental breach it is necessary 'to look at the events which had occurred as a result of the breach' and to decide whether their effect had been to 'deprive the party not in default of substantially the whole benefit which it was intended that he should obtain from the contract.' "[76]

The starting point was the decision of the House of Lords in *Haine* v. *Tate & Lyle*.[77] In that case, after a deviation had occurred, a charterer had acted in a manner which suggested an affirmation of the contract of affreightment and a waiver of the shipowner's breach. In these circumstances, the House of Lords held that the shipowner's deviation had not automatically terminated the contract, since that would have permitted a wrongdoer the right unilaterally to determine his contract and thus possibly profit from his wrongdoing.[78] Instead, the House treated this as any other breach. The deviation constituted a form of repudiation which the charterer then had the option either to accept, and thus terminate the contract, or ignore, and thus waive the breach and affirm the contract but at the same time reserving the right to damages, and this is what the charterer had done. Both Lord Atkin and Lord Wright spoke of this deviation from the contract route as a fundamental breach of contract[79] and this was later seized upon by Devlin J. in 1951 in his judgment in *Chandris* v. *Isbrandstsen-Moller*.[80]

This case concerned a claim for demurrage in circumstances in which a charterer had loaded a dangerous cargo in breach of contract, with the result that unloading was delayed. In his judgment Devlin J. referred to breach of "some fundamental or basic condition of the contract, such as is involved, for example, in a deviation from the contract voyage," and he cited *Hain* v. *Tate & Lyle* in support.[81] In the same passage he also referred to deviation as a "fundamental breach going to the root of the contract." It is by no means clear, however, that Devlin J. meant by this terminology anything more than an ordinary condition going to the root of the contract, the breach of which entitles the other party to repudiate.

A few months later Devlin J. reiterated this proposition in a more precise form. In *Alexander* v. *Railway Executive*[82] the plaintiff went with an associate called Colmar to deposit luggage at a railway station. Colmar on a later occasion induced one of the defendant's clerks to let him open the cases and remove some of their contents; later still he persuaded the clerk to let him take the cases away and he absconded with them. The contract of deposit contained an exemption clause. Devlin J. said[83]:

"I think that that must be said to be a fundamental breach of contract. ... The ordinary law of contract ... involves that, where there has been a breach of a fundamental term

of a contract giving the other party the right to rescind it,
then, unless and until, with full knowledge of all the facts,
he elects to affirm the contract and not rescind it, the
special terms of the contract go and cannot be relied upon
by the defaulting party.''

There is some confusion of terminology in the passage
quoted. Devlin J. talks of ''fundamental breach'' and
''breach of a fundamental term'' as describing the same situation; he speaks of ''the right to rescind'' when perhaps he
means the right to repudiate. However, it is fairly clear that
he regards the ''fundamental breach'' that occurred in this
case as something different from the total failure of consideration that has earlier in this chapter been characterised as
breach of a fundamental term, because he speaks of the
injured party having an option to ''rescind'' or affirm the
contract. If Devlin J. had in mind breach of a fundamental
term, there would of course be nothing of the old contract to
affirm, only an entirely new one to be concluded by acceptance of the promisor's offer, made in the form of his default.
In this new contract, the offeree's obligation would presumably be to pay a reasonable sum on a *quantum meruit* or a
quantum valebant, in which case the exclusion clause could
have no application anyway, since the reasonableness of the
sum due would have to be judged in the light of the value of
the performance actually rendered.

This new doctrine of fundamental breach, then, appeared
to be nothing more than an ordinary breach of contract
having especially serious consequences for the promisee but
permitting him, providing he repudiated the contract, to sue
the promisor in contract for damages, any exclusion clause
notwithstanding. At this stage, however, it appeared to be a
term to cover the *post-Hain* case type of deviation in contracts
of carriage and cognate breaches in other types of bailment.
Indeed, in *The Albion*[84] the Court of Appeal decided that

the concept was limited to breaches in the nature of a deviation. Somervell L.J. said[85]: "We have referred to these cases (the then existing authorities on fundamental breach) because we think that the words 'fundamental breach' might be read in this context in a wider sense than the decisions justify." It was, therefore, left to Denning L.J. to extend this new concept of fundamental breach out of this narrow area into the general field of commercial law and the particular area of consumer protection; he did this in a case in 1956 involving hire-purchase of a motor vehicle, the case of *Karsales (Harrow) Ltd.* v. *Wallis.*[86]

In this case the defendant was shown a second-hand Buick in excellent condition, and he wished to acquire it. Arrangements were made with a finance company for hire-purchase and the agreement contained a clause excluding liability for breach of conditions or warranties of any description. After the contract had been concluded the car was towed, at night, to the defendant's premises. It was in a very poor state indeed; many detachable parts had been detached, new parts had been replaced by old, the engine was so defective that towing was the only means of propulsion and, not surprisingly, the defendant refused to accept or pay for it. He was sued by the plaintiffs who were the assignees of the finance company. Birkett L.J.[87] and Parker L.J.[88] both held that the plaintiffs could not rely on the exclusion clause because they had not performed their contract at all — a car had not been delivered, the consideration had totally failed and the defendant could repudiate the contract and set up the plaintiff's breach of a fundamental term as a defence to the action. Denning L.J. was not, however, prepared to go this far. He did not talk in terms of a complete non-performance but instead talked of "a breach which goes to the root of the contract."[89] He seemed to take the view that even where the breach of contract was not sufficiently serious to amount to a complete non-performance of the obligations contracted for, nevertheless an exclusion clause may still not apply as a rule of law where the breach caused serious loss to the defendant. However, instead of construing both the positive and negative terms together to ascertain whether the owner had fulfilled his undertakings, as was done in the *Hain* case, Denning L.J. adopted the earlier cannons of construction:

> "The thing to do is to look at the contract *apart from the exemption clause* and see what are the terms, express or implied, which impose an obligation on the party. If he has been guilty of a breach of those obligations in a respect which goes to the very root of the contract, he cannot rely on the exempting clauses."[90]

So breach of a fundamental term was equivalent to non-performance; fundamental breach was simply breach, but with fundamental consequences. The difference in effect between the two was that in the case of breach of a fundamental term the contract terminates automatically. In the case of fundamental breach the contract survives unless repudiated. The innocent party can thus either repudiate the contract, in which case the authorities suggested that the exclusion clause would not protect the party in breach, or he can affirm the contract and simply sue for compensation for his loss. However, logic would dictate that if he affirms the contract he affirms all the contract, including the exclusion clause, so that the question of whether his claim for compensation is successful would depend, *inter alia,* upon whether the exclusion clause, on its construction, covers the breach that had occurred.[91]

Considerable doubt was thrown on this last proposition, however, as a result of a decision of the Court of Appeal in *Charterhouse Credit Co. Ltd.* v. *Tolly.*[92] This case again concerned the hire-purchase of a motor vehicle that was supplied with a serious rear-axle defect costing between £40 and £50 to repair. However, instead of rejecting the car when the defect was discovered, the defendant affirmed the contract and in the action brought against him by the finance company he successfully counterclaimed for damages, despite the presence of an exclusion clause. The main problem with this result is that it does not conform to the view expressed by the House of Lords in *Hain* v. *Tate & Lyle*[93] that a fundamental breach operates as any other breach of contract. If there has been a fundamental breach and the injured party nevertheless chooses to affirm the contract, as in fact happened in *Charterhouse Credit* v. *Tolly,* [94] then surely the whole contract should be affirmed, including the exclusion clause. However, the Court of Appeal took a different view, holding that where there has been a fundamental breach of contract, regardless of whether the innocent party affirms or repudiates, an exclusion clause can never, as a matter of law, protect the party in breach.

It is essentially this notion upon which the House of Lords launch an attack in the leading case of *Suisse Atlantique Société d'Armement Maritime S.A.* v. *N.V. Rotterdamsche Kolen Centrale.*[95] This case did not really raise the issue of an exclusion clause at all. The respondents chartered boats from the appellants for a certain period of time to carry coal from America to Europe. The charterparty laid down a specified rate at which the boat was to be loaded, since the owners' remuneration was to turn on the number of voyages made. The charterparty contained a clause stating that if the charterers took longer to load than the number of days specified, the charterers were to pay demurrage at the rate of $1,000 per day. The appellants complained that, because the charterers delayed in loading, they lost freight charges in respect of a possible six voyages. They could have claimed that this was a breach going to the root of the contract and repudiated. They did not. Instead they carried on with the charterparty and then claimed, not the $1,000 a day demurrage, but the money they had lost in freight. Normally demurrage would be considered as a pre-estimate of damages, not as an exclusion clause at all.[96] However, the appellants said that they were not bound by the pre-estimate since the clause was in reality an exemption from paying damages for loss of freight. Thus it was alleged that since the detention of the vessel beyond the laydays was a fundamental breach of the charterparty, the respondents were unable to rely on the demurrage clause to limit their liability, even though the contract had been affirmed.

A majority of the House of Lords rejected the contention that the demurrage clause was an exemption, treating it instead as a genuine pre-estimate of damages that should be upheld. However their Lordships (although it could be argued that their deliberations are strictly *obiter*) proceeded to review the law on fundamental breach. After the decision of the Court of Appeal in *Charterhouse Credit Co. Ltd.* v. *Tolly*[97] it was thought that an exclusion clause, however widely drawn, could not protect a contracting party who had committed a fundamental breach of contract, even if the contract had been affirmed. Such a rule was given the force of a rule of law. The House of Lords, whilst not specifically overruling *Tolly's* case, reject this doctrine, preferring the view of Pearson L.J. expressed in *U.G.S. Finance* v. *National Mortgage Bank of Greece*[98]:

"As to the question of 'fundamental', I think there is a rule of construction that normally an exception or an exclusion clause or similar provision in a contract should be construed as not applying to a situation created by a fundamental breach of contract. This is not an independent rule of law imposed by the court on the parties willy-nilly in disregard of their contractual intention. On the contrary it is a rule of construction based on the presumed intention of the contracting parties. It involves the implication of a term to give to the contract that business efficacy which the parties as reasonable men must have intended it to have. This rule of construction is not new in principle but it has become prominent in recent years in consequence of the tendency to have standard forms of contract containing exception clauses drawn in extravagantly wide terms, which would produce absurd results if applied literally.''

So, it appears that there is no rule of substantive law to the effect that a party cannot contract out of, or limit, his liability for fundamental breach. As a device for protecting consumers the doctrine might have worked quite well, but it was liable at the same time to upset perfectly fair bargains between businessmen for the reasonable allocation of contractual risks, although, as will be seen, the new approach is likely to have a similar effect. The doctrine of fundamental breach, it was said, should be a rule of construction only.[99] This rule of construction operates to prevent an exclusion clause being applied literally if that would lead to an absurdity,[1] or where there is a "strong though rebuttable presumption" that the parties did not intend the clause to cover fundamental breaches,[2] or where the clause is not drawn in terms wide enough to cover "a total breach."[3] Since the rule is a rule of construction it can be displaced by sufficiently clear words in the contract itself.

On a question of principle, the House of Lords appear to conclude that there is no difference in operation between a fundamental breach and a breach of condition. It simply involves a type of breach which gives to the innocent party an option to affirm or repudiate. Faced with a fundamental breach the innocent party can either repudiate on the spot, and cease to be bound, or he must affirm. This is the only way a breach can operate.[4] If he repudiates, the whole contract ceases to exist, including the exemption clause. Whether the clause can, in this circumstance, still be used to prevent the innocent party recovering in damages that which he has lost through the breach is another question. There is authority that it cannot,[5] although this question is discussed in more detail below. If the innocent party affirms the contract, the clause excluding liability continues to apply. In those cases where the contract is affirmed and yet the exclusion clause is still held not to apply, this is because, on its construction, the exclusion clause does not cover the breach in question. Even where, on its construction, it does so cover the breach, it may still be held to be unreasonable, and thus invalid, under the provisions of the Unfair Contract Terms Act 1977, which is discussed later. The point to be stressed as a result of the *Suisse Atlantique* decision, however, is that there is no rule of the common law that an exclusion clause can *never* apply in the event of a fundamental breach.

There are certain circumstances, this principle notwithstanding, where an exclusion clause, on its construction, will not apply. These were characterised by Lord Reid as falling under four heads[6]:

(a)   where the clause is not wide enough to cover the kind of breach committed;
(b)   where the terms of the clause are so wide that they cannot be applied literally;
(c)   where the clause leads to absurdity;
(d)   where the clause would defeat the main object of the contract.

This probably means that, on their construction, very few exemption clauses could be construed to cover the event of a fundamental breach.[7] In *Wathes* (*Western*) *Ltd.* v. *Austins* (*Menswear*) *Ltd,*[8] the plaintiffs supplied and installed an air conditioning plant in the defendants' shop under a contract, clause 14 of which purported to exempt the plaintiffs from liability for any consequential-loss damages claims. The plant was so noisy in its operation that the owners of the next-door shop issued a writ against the defendants on a claim for nuisance. The defendants, under this threat, undertook work at their own expense to abate the nuisance and when sued by the plaintiffs for the contract price counterclaimed for the cost of the abatement work together with their costs for compromising the nuisance action. The plaintiffs relied on the exclusion clause. The defendants had not, of course, repudiated the contract, but affirmed it, deciding instead to take remedial action and claim damages. Both Megaw L.J. and Sir John Pennycuick[9] did not regard the decision in *Tolly's* case as having been overruled by *Suisse Atlantique* but instead placed upon it the gloss that, unless express words are used, an exemption clause will not cover liability in the event of a fundamental breach. It is implicit in the Court of Appeal's decision that, as a matter of construction, it will be difficult, if not impossible, to exclude liability for fundamental breach by a suitably-worded clause. If words sufficiently precise are used, words that actually mention fundamental breach, or talk of breaches "going to the root of the contract," or describe in detail especially disastrous consequences for which the promisor is not to be liable, it is likely then that the clause will be disallowed as being too wide, or as defeating the main object of the contract.

The degree of the courts' reluctance to construe a clause as protecting the party in breach will be directly proportional to the seriousness of that breach, which in turn depends upon the seriousness of the consequences for the innocent party. Where the breach is fundamental the consequences will be more serious than for a breach of condition and the courts will be more reluctant to adopt a liberal construction of the clause. This point was made by Donaldson J. in *Kenyon Son & Craven Ltd.* v. *Baxter Hoare & Co. Ltd.*[10] In this case bags of peanuts stored in the defendants' warehouse were seriously damaged as a result of rat infestation. The defendants were aware of the infestation and informed the local authority but no successful control procedures were instituted.

The contract between the parties contained a clause excluding liability for loss or damage to goods in the defendants' custody or control "unless such loss or damage is due to the wilful neglect or default" of the defendants or their servants; and a further clause limited the defendants' liability to a specified sum. The plaintiffs attempted to claim compensation from the defendants in respect of the damaged nuts, and were met by the limitation clauses. Donaldson J. held that the defendants had not been guilty of a fundamental breach and that on its true construction the clause protected the defendants against an ordinary breach since the loss had occurred as a result of carelessness but not recklessness, and it would only be recklessness that would fall within the "wilful neglect or default" provision of the clause.[11] However, he then considered what would have been the position " ... assuming that I am wrong that the defendants were guilty of a fundamental breach."[12] As an ordinary breach of condition, the clause on its construction covered the breach but a far more stringent approach was to be adopted if the breach was more serious. If the warehousemen had committed a fundamental breach by, for example, storing the nuts in a cellar, or in the open air, then the clause would not have protected them.

Their Lordships in the *Suisse Atlantique* case do not, however, see any reason why a contract should not make provision for events which the parties do not have in contemplation, or even events which are unforeseeable,[13] if sufficiently clear words are used. Nevertheless, a fundamental breach can only operate so as to allow the plaintiff to repudiate if he wishes at common law and cease to be bound, or to affirm and take his chance on the construction of the exemption clause.

F. *The Option to Affirm or Repudiate*

Although this option to affirm or repudiate is the only way in which a fundamental breach can operate, there may well be cases where this is impossible, *i.e.* although in theory the innocent party has an option where there has been a fundamental breach, in practice he does not learn about the breach until the contract has been performed, when it is too late to repudiate. The problem then facing the court is whether it can look back to the time for the breach and hold that the innocent party did elect to terminate the contract, because, had he known of the breach at the time it was committed, he would undoubtedly have terminated, since this would have been the only sensible and reasonable thing to do. Alternatively the court could simply hold that since the contract has been completed it must be taken as having been affirmed, and that therefore the "innocent" party's fate will be decided on the construction of the exclusion clause.

The indications in the *Suisse Atlantique* case are in favour of the former approach. Lord Upjohn said[14]:

"In very many ... cases ... there was no question of any election by the innocent party either to affirm or disaffirm the contract when the other party had committed a fundamental breach. This is because in so many cases ... the voyage or journey or warehousing contract has been completed before the innocent party gets to know of any breaches of it, and the only course open to him is to sue for breach, and he does so upon the footing that he is entitled to treat the whole contract as at an end, for the law is clear that where there has been a fundamental breach he can only be taken to affirm the contract if he knows his full rights."[15]

This problem arose directly in *Harbutts Plasticine Ltd.* v. *Wayne Tank and Pump Co. Ltd.*[16] In this case the defendants agreed with the plaintiffs to design, and install in the plaintiff's factory, equipment for storing and dispensing stearine (a substance used in the manufacture of plasticine) in in a molten state. To maintain the stearine at the required temperature it was necessary to heat the storage tanks and the delivery pipes that connected up to the processing plant. The pipe was heated by means of a special electrical tape wound round the pipe, but, on the defendants' advice, this delivery pipe was itself made of a plastic material called "durapipe." "Durapipe" was totally unsuitable for the purpose. It was liable to soften at a temperature of 187°F. and the stearine within the pipe had to be maintained at 160°F. Since the plastic pipe was a poor conductor of heat, it was not certain that the internal temperature of 160°F. could be attained without exceeding an external temperature on the pipe of 187°F. Again, since the pipe was a poor conductor of heat, the temperature could not be properly regulated by the thermostat placed in contact with the pipe. For the purpose of testing the system, one of the defendants' employees switched on the heating system in the evening to let it warm up overnight, ready for the next day. Overnight the exterior of the pipe overheated before the interior reached 160°f. and in the absence of an effective thermostatic regulation, the external temperature continued to rise until the pipe disintegrated, allowing the highly inflammable stearine to come into contact with the heating tape. It caught fire, but worse was yet in store since, in the absence of overnight supervision, the fire spread and the plaintiff's factory was burned down. The contract contained a clause limiting liability for accidents and damage before takeover of the plant to the contract price of £2,300. The plaintiffs, however, understandably no doubt, in the circumstances, wanted compensation to enable them to rebuild the factory.

The plaintiffs alleged that there had been a fundamental breach of the contract in that the supply of the "durapipe," which was wholly unsuitable for the job, went to the very root of the contract. None of the judges doubted this contention. Lord Denning M.R. thought that on a construction of the exemption clause it was confined to limiting liability to damage or accidents done in the course of erecting the plant, *i.e.* when the damage was a result of the defendants' negligence. He did not think it contemplated protecting the defendants from breaches of contract, because these occurred without the negligence of anyone.[17] However, in case he was wrong about this he based his decision on the much wider ground adopted by Widgery and Cross L.JJ.,[18] which assumed that the clause could apply to contractual breaches.

All three members of the Court consider the problem mentioned by Lord Upjohn in the *Suisse Atlantique* case.[19] There is one type of fundamental breach which leaves the contract still open to further performance. The innocent party still has a real option to affirm or terminate the contract. If he elects to affirm it, then it remains in being for the future on both sides. The exemption clause survives and may or may not cover the breach on its construction. There is another type of fundamental breach, however, which itself brings the contract to an end since there is no room, in reality, for an option to be given to the innocent party, if one assumes him to be a reasonable man who would take the only sensible commercial course open to him. This is not the same as breach of a fundamental term,[20] which, as we have seen, amounts to a total non-performance; it is merely seriously defective performance amounting to a breach, with disastrous consequences for the other party. The *Harbutts Plasticine* case is a good example of this type of fundamental breach. The fire was so disastrous that it destroyed the factory. Through the fault of the defendants the contract was in effect terminated since no reasonable man would affirm the contract when the entire factory had been burned to the ground. It was as if the contract had come to an end by an event which, had it occurred without fault, in the sense of breach, would have been regarded as a frustrating event, terminating the contract without either side having an election to continue it.[21] The contract, of necessity, should therefore be treated as terminated.

G. *The Effects of Termination*

In the *Harbutts Plasticine* case the Court of Appeal, on the authority of *Suisse Atlantique,* held that since it has been repudiated, the whole contract falls and with it falls the exclusion clause, so that it no longer protects the party in breach, who must consequently compensate the plaintiffs for the loss of the factory. This is an approach which the Court of Appeal repeated a few months later in *Farnworth Finance Facilities Ltd.* v. *Attryde.*[22] The plaintiff finance company bought a new motorbike from the dealers and hired it to the defendant under a hire-purchase agreement. The agreement excluded all conditions, express or implied, save those implied under the Hire-Purchase Act 1965. After the hirer took delivery of the bike it gave a great deal of trouble and it was returned both to the dealers and the manufacturers for repair. During this repair period the hirer continued to pay the instalments. Finally, when the chain broke and shattered the crank case, the hirer stopped the payments and returned the machine. The plaintiff finance company brought an action for recovery of the balance of the hire-purchase charges and sought to defend the hirer's counterclaim by reliance on the exclusion clause. The Court of Appeal held that the defects in the bike were so serious as to render it totally unsafe for the road, and this constituted a fundamental breach of contract. The Court of Appeal further held that the hirer had merely used the machine for a reasonable period of time in order to ascertain the full extent of the defects.[23] When he did discover them he rejected it. So, there was no affirmation of the contract. Lord Denning M.R. took the view, on the authority of the *Harbutts Plasticine* case,[24] that since the contract was repudiated, the whole contract fell, including the exclusion, and the plaintiffs could not therefore rely on it.

This idea appears to derive from a suggestion of Lord Reid in the *Suisse Atlantique* case, where he said[25]:

> "If fundamental breach is established, the next question is what effect, if any, that has on the applicability of other terms of the contract. This question has often arisen with regard to clauses excluding liability, in whole or in part, of the party in breach. I do not think that there is generally much difficulty when the innocent party has elected to treat the breach as a repudiation, bring the contract to an end and sue for damages. Then the whole contract has ceased to exist including the exclusion clause, and I do not see how that clause can then be used to exclude an action for loss which will be suffered by the innocent party after it has ceased to exist, such as loss of the profit which would have accrued if the contract had run its full term."

There are grave problems with this approach.[26] It seems to suggest that if the contract is repudiated the whole contract falls, apart from the cause of action giving rise to the claim for damages. It is by no means clear whether repudiation for fundamental breach is repudiation *ab initio*, from the time of the breach, from the time when it became fundamental or from the time of the election to repudiate. This time factor seemed to concern Megaw L.J. greatly in *Wathes* (*Western*) *Ltd.* v. *Austins* (*Menswear*) *Ltd.*[27] The usual contractual rule is that when a contract ends as a result of frustration, or election to repudiate, it ends at the moment the frustrating event occurs, or the election is made. Until such time the contract remains valid and binding and all its terms continue to operate as agreed between the parties. Hence the innocent party may sue the other for breach of a contract which was terminated for that breach, because at the moment of that breach the contract was in force. Hence, rights and liabilities which arise before termination are not destroyed. So, neither frustration nor election to disaffirm can avoid a contract *ab initio*, but can only put an end to future rights and liabilities. The issue was put with his customary lucidity by Dixon J. in the Australian High Court in *McDonald* v. *Dennys Lascelles Limited*[28]:

> "When a party to a simple contract, upon a breach by the other contracting party of a condition of the contract, elects to treat the contract as no longer binding upon him, the contract is not rescinded from the beginning. Both parties are discharged from the further performance of the contract, but rights are not divested or discharged which have already been unconditionally acquired. Rights and obligations which arise from the partial execution of the contract and causes of action which have accrued from its breach alike continue unaffected. When a contract is rescinded because of matters which affect its formation, as in the case of fraud, the parties are to be rehabilitated and restored, so far as may be, to the position they occupied before the contract was made. But when a contract, which is not void or voidable at law, or liable to be set aside in equity, is dissolved at the election of one party because the other has not observed an essential condition or has committed a breach going to its root, the contract is determined so far as it is executory only and the party in default is liable for damages for its breach."

If a fundamental breach only operates as does any other kind of repudiatory breach, *i.e.* to give an option to affirm or disaffirm, why should the rule as to termination be any different from that pertaining to any other repudiatory breach? Any other result would be illogical. If the repudiation *ante-*dates the breach, then presumably one must regard the contract as ceasing to exist at a time before the breach occurred, in which case, whilst there may be a claim for the return of money paid in quasi contract, there can be no surviving cause of action in contract on which to base a claim for damages. If the repudiation *post*-dates the breach, as needs it must to give rise to a contractual claim, then, presumably, at the time the cause of action accrued, the contract, including the exclusion clause, was still standing and therefore the success or otherwise of the "innocent" party's claim to damages ought to be determined by whether or not the exclusion clause can be construed to cover the breach that has occurred in just the same way as it would if he had affirmed. This is the only way that one can comply with the view expressed by the House of Lords that the doctrine of fundamental breach should not be treated as a rule of law, but should be regarded as a doctrine of construction only. On this point, then, the decisions of the Court of Appeal reached after 1967 that take a different line, and which have been discussed in this section, cannot be supported.

It is not difficult to see how this misinterpretation arose. As was explained earlier in this Chapter, the bailment and deviation cases were originally regarded as cases of total failure of consideration — breach of a fundamental term. So, the effect of automatic repudiation in these cases was to leave the promissee free to recover, not on the contract, but either in quasi-contract for the return of monies paid, or by virtue of some concurrent liability, such as breach of the duty of care in bailment. Once the House of Lords decided in *Hain* v. *Tate & Lyle*[29] that a deviation did not amount to a total failure of consideration but a breach operating as any other repudiatory breach, then the unreality of permitting actions for damages in the absence of a special rule of law became more apparent. Treating a deviation as any other breach emphasised the fact that, in strict law, liability in contract and any concurrent liability ought, in the first instance, to be governed by the construction of any exclusion clause that was still existing at the time of the breach. This would not matter, of course, as long as the fundamental breach doctrine was allowed to operate as a rule of law which in some mysterious way or other disallowed the exclusion clause whilst leaving the guilty party's other contractual obligations intact. Once the doctrine was recognised as being a matter of construction only, then it became difficult to see why the innocent party should be better off, *vis-à-vis* the exclusion clause, by repudiating than he would be by affirming.

The Unfair Contract Terms Act 1977 attempts to deal with this problem by a combination of two provisions. First, where one of the parties to a contract deals as a consumer or deals on the other's written terms of business and that contract contains an exclusion clause, then that clause cannot be relied upon "except in so far as" it "satisfied the requirement of reasonableness." For this purpose, an exclusion clause is any clause which[30]:

(a) excludes or restricts the liability of the party in breach *in respect of that breach*; (this provision expressly preserves the rule of construction, which must be applied before the statutory provision as to reasonableness. It is only by construing the clause that the court can decide whether the clause operates "in respect of the breach" at all. Part, at least, then of the fundamental breach doctrine as a matter of construction survives);
or

(b) permits the promisor to render a contractual performance substantially different from that which was reasonably expected of him;
or

(c) permits the promisor in respect of the whole or any part of his contractual obligation, to render no performance at all.

Section 13 decrees that any term which makes any liability or its enforcement subject to restrictive or onerous conditions, or which excludes or restricts a right or remedy in respect of liability, or subjects any person to any prejudice in consequence of his pursuing any such right or remedy (for example a "blacklist"), or which excludes or restricts rules of evidence or procedure (such as attempting to reverse the normal burden of proof, or providing that particular conduct will be deemed to be conclusive evidence of a fact), are all exclusion clauses and thus subject to the controls of the Act. These are not easy provisions to grasp. As to (a), the approach the courts adopt to contractual interpretation will determine whether it has any effect. Where lies the difference, for instance, in terms of what is promised, between an undertaking to supply a Brooklands 2,000 G.T. model in red, but "liability for breach of all conditions and warranties, express or implied, is hereby excluded," and an undertaking "to supply a motor vehicle, the make, engine capacity, model and colour to be selected by the vendor on the advice, which need not be followed, of the purchaser"? If the purchaser advises that he would like a Brooklands 2,000 G.T. model in red and, after listening to this advice, the vendor chooses to supply a Brooklands 1,500 saloon in blue, the purchaser can presumably challenge the exclusion clause if drafted as in our first example, but in the second there is nothing to challenge under (a) at all, even though in essence the obligations under both contracts are the same.

Perhaps the second contract can be caught by (b), *i.e.* as a term under which the promisor claims "to be entitled to render a contractual performance substantially different from that which was reasonably expected of him," although why the promisor should be expected, in our example, to do more than supply a car and listen to (but not necessarily follow) the advice of the purchaser it is difficult to see. It may be that terms such as those found in our second example, leaving the choice of goods to the seller with no obligation to follow the buyer's advice, could be treated as an exclusion, and thus subject to the test of reasonableness. This may be so by virtue of section 13(1)(*a*), in that they might be seen as making the seller's liability, or the enforcement of it, subject to "restrictive or onerous conditions." However, since the form of words used results in the seller having no liability at all in respect of those matters about which the buyer is likely to complain, it is difficult to understand how any "liability," or its consequent enforcement, is being made subject to any conditions at all, let alone onerous ones. In any event, unlike reasonableness, "restrictive or onerous conditions" are nowhere defined in the Act and the Courts are thus left with a virtually unfettered discretion in this regard.[31] So far as (c) is concerned, it has already been pointed out in Chapter 4 that a contract under which the promisor is under no obligation to perform at all is, in reality an illusory contract and should be struck down for want of consideration. The problem really turns on the question discussed at length in Chapter 4. Are exclusion clauses really just defences or are they negative statements of positive obligation? Section 3 of the Act, by attempting to deal only with certain clauses by reference to criteria of reasonableness, would seem to make it virtually certain that the proponents of the "defence" theory win the day.

The second provision of the Act aimed primarily at fundamental breach is that contained in section 9. This provides that if the clause is one to which the reasonableness doctrine applies, then the mere fact that the contract has been terminated would not, by itself, result in the exclusion clause having no effect. However, it is still open to the court to construe the exclusion clause as not applying to the breach that has occurred, so that there would then be no question of having to consider the matter of reasonableness at all. Also, the provision preventing automatic invalidity on termination only applies to clauses which are affected by the reasonableness doctrine, *i.e.* certain clauses excluding or restricting liability for negligence, certain exemption clauses in standard form contracts or contracts to which one of the parties is a consumer, indemnity clauses in consumer contracts,[32] clauses excluding or restricting liability for breach of the implied terms in sections 13, 14, or 15 of the Sale of Goods Act 1893 or sections 9, 10 or 11 of the Supply of Goods (Implied Terms) Act 1973 in non-consumer transactions,[33] and similar implied terms under various miscellaneous contracts under which goods pass (*e.g.* contracts for work and materials).[34] Also so subject are clauses purporting to exclude or restrict liability for any remedy available for misrepresentation. In all other cases, then,[35] the old common law rules relating to fundamental breach will continue to apply in full including the anomalous provision making the exclusion clause of no effect when the contract is repudiated. Section 9(2) provides that where the contract is affirmed on a breach this will not, of course, prevent the application of the reasonableness requirement. Although it is not expressly stated, this, presumably, will only be in relation to those clauses which otherwise qualify for the application of the reasonableness doctrine under the Act.

There are, therefore, several types of contract, largely specially negotiated commercial contracts between businessmen that are not "back of order" or standard form, where the risks are likely to have been carefully assessed and costed, where the Act will not apply and the common law rules of fundamental breach will apply in their full rigour. Also, because the Act appears to preserve the rules of construction as the first step in dealing with exclusion clauses, the fundamental breach doctrine remains of vital importance since, as a result of the view taken by the Court of Appeal of the *Suisse Atlantique* decision, the question of whether or not there has been a fundamental breach is a vital factor in the construction of the clause. It might, perhaps, have been better had the clause been a vital factor in deciding whether there has been a fundamental breach.

H. *The Effects of Affirmation*

It has been suggested[36] that a party who affirms the contract will be bound by an exclusion clause in the event of a fundamental breach. It is hard to understand why this should necessarily be so in the case of affirmation any more than it should necessarily not be so in the case of repudiation. The question in every case should be one of construing the exclusion clause to ascertain whether or not it covers the breach which has occurred.[37] Having done that, the Unfair Contract Terms Act then requires in many cases, which have already been discussed elsewhere in this work, the clause to satisfy the test of reasonableness. Indeed, if Lord Denning M.R. is correct, the common law imposes a requirement of reasonableness without the assistance of statute, at least in relation to standard form contracts.[38] However, the primary task is that of construction, since it is that exercise that will determine whether or not the clause covers the breach. If it does not cover the breach we have no need of reasonableness notions at all. There is little point, though, in denying the existence of a rule of law for termination, only to impose one for affirmation. In both instances the problem of whether or not the clause can be construed to cover a fundamental breach should be determined by reference to those principles discussed in Chapter 4.

It will be remembered that in *Charterhouse Credit Co. Ltd.* v. *Tolly*[39] the Court of Appeal held that a hirer who affirmed after a fundamental breach was, as a matter of law, not bound by the exemption clause. Although *Tolly's* case was not specifically overruled by the House of Lords, it might have been thought to be a difficult decision to follow now on the question of affirmation. Nevertheless Lord Denning M.R. has attempted in various *obiter dicta* to revive the rule of law expounded in *Tolly's* case in the guise of a rule of construction. In *Farnworth Finance Facilities Ltd.* v. *Attryde*[40] he observed that even if the hirer had affirmed the contract, the exclusion clause could not apply because of the fundamental breach. In *Anglo-Continental Holidays Ltd.* v. *Typaldos Lines Ltd.*[41] he said: "No matter how wide the terms of the clause, the court will limit and modify it to the extent necessary to enable effect to be given to the main object and intent of the contract." Lord Denning M.R. has made similar remarks in other cases.[42] He has recently found some support from a differently constituted Court of Appeal under Megaw L.J. in *Wathes (Western) Ltd.* v. *Austins (Menswear) Ltd.*[43] There, although the court took the view that the clause was not applicable "as a matter of construction," it really seemed to proceed on the basis of what the result would have been had the contract been repudiated. By applying the decision in *Harbutts Plasticine* it was forced to come to the conclusion that the exclusion clause would then not have applied. From this it reasoned that the result should be no different in the event of affirmation. The logic was impeccable but, as it has been our endeavour to show, the premise was unsound. Megaw L.J. even cited with approval the decision in *Tolly's* case, and suggested that he was bound by it.[44] These statements cannot really represent the law. They are clearly inconsistent with the *Suisse Atlantique* decision which, if it does nothing else, emphasises that if an exclusion clause is drafted with a sufficient degree of care and precision and, one must now add, is found to be reasonable, it can be construed to relieve a party otherwise guilty of a fundamental breach, at least where the contract has been affirmed.

I. *The Distinction Between a Fundamental Breach and Other Breaches of Contract*

This problem is discussed at some length by the Court of Appeal in the *Harbutts Plasticine* case[45] and at similar length but with rather less precision in the *Wathes (Western)* case.[46] Both cases, however, make the point that when one is dealing with breach of a fundamental term, it is the character of the performance proferred, in relation to the term broken, that is the operative factor; in the case of fundamental breach, one is concerned with the consequences of the breach, not the quality of the act constituting the breach, or the importance of the term broken. The Courts of Appeal in both cases refer to the judgment of Diplock L.J. in *Hong Kong Fir Shipping Co. Ltd.* v. *Kawasaki Kisen Kaisha Ltd.*[47] The essence of Diplock L.J.'s view is that it is not the term itself, but the effects of its breach, that are important. The real issue should be whether the consequences of the breach deprive the innocent party of substantially the whole benefit of the contract which it was intended he should obtain. If the contract is broken in a way that causes serious loss, it should be treated as a repudiatory breach, but if it is broken in a way that only causes trifling loss, then its breach will not justify termination.[48]

Adopting this analysis in the *Harbutts Plasticine* case, it follows that the first step is to see whether an "event" has occurred which has deprived the innocent party of substantially the whole benefit of the contract. The fire was such an event because not only did it destroy the equipment installed by the defendants but it destroyed the factory as well. That being so, the breach, occasioned by specifying the wrong type of pipe, was a repudiatory breach. A breach will be repudiatory if the consequences of it are more than slight or trifling. It will be a fundamental breach if the consequences are so serious as to deprive the innocent party of substantially the whole benefit of the contract. A serious breach may have slight consequences; a trivial breach grave ones. For instance, the breach of contract in the *Harbutts Plasticine* case was the specification of durapipe. However, had the problem been discovered in time and the pipe been replaced by a stainless steel one, it is highly unlikely that the plaintiffs would have been permitted to treat the contract as at an end. Suppose the problem had been discovered after a small fire had broken out but the fire had been brought under control and little permanent damage was done. This might or might not have been regarded as a repudiatory breach but it would not have been a fundamental breach. In fact the breach in this case had disastrous consequences for the plaintiffs; not only did it deprive them of the entire benefit under the contract, it destroyed the entire factory: the breach was therefore fundamental. Widgery L.J. suggests[49] that if the event which occurred as a result of the guilty party's breach is an event which would have frustrated the contract had it occurred without the fault of either party, then the breach will be a fundamental breach if it occurs with fault.

There are, however, certain factors which make this approach a far from ideal one. It will be recalled that in Chapter 1 we saw that the lack of confidence expressed by the business community in legal solutions to their problems stemmed partly from a mistrust of the lawyers approach to commercial matters. Also, where large sums of money were at stake, or where the liability for consequential loss was great, or where the contract involved the disposal of goods of great complexity, contracts, especially the clauses dealing with the allocation of risk, were planned with meticulous care. Contracts were costed, or insurance cover was taken out, on the basis of this allocation. Standard forms or "back of order" terms were used, partially at least, because of the business confidence that familiarity with regular courses of dealing engendered. The modern approach of both legislature and judiciary is to leave until after the contract is made, indeed until after there has been a breach, the question of deciding what force will be given to certain contractual terms. If the question of whether a breach should or should not be regarded as repudiatory turns upon the consequences flowing from that breach, it becomes extremely difficult for the parties or their advisors to predict what their respective risks are likely to be. No commercial man minds a race — even an obstacle race — but he might well resent a contest in which the tape is moved further away from him the nearer he gets to it, and in which the stewards are constantly moving the obstacles around the course. The practical result of the "consequences" approach must be to make it harder for parties who are negotiating for the supply of goods and services, and who formerly covered themselves by exclusion clauses and insurance, to predict the consequences of their agreement. What is essential for business is that the parties are able to plan rational safeguards, by means of exclusion and limitation clauses and consequent insurance cover, together with negotiations over price, for the risks they undertake. This requires an allocation of risks and allocation of the respective insurable interests, before the contract. Whatever may be the merits for the ordinary consumer, whose interests are, in any event, as it is hoped to demonstrate in the next chapter, better served by *separate* legislation, the business community's undertakings are not assisted in their fulfilment by imposing, after the accident or breach, *ex post facto* tests to determine whether the effects of the event were sufficiently serious to warrant repudiation, if the result is to upset the risks as allocated by the parties.[50]

There is, in addition, the further difficulty of the time factor. It would be unfortunate if a victim of a breach of contract, uncertain whether the breach is serious enough to entitle him to repudiate, hangs fire and thus loses his right to reject[51] or proceeds to repudiate only to find himself in breach because the court subsequently holds that the events which flowed from the other party's failure to comply with this term were not serious enough to warrant repudiation. The problem was summed up by Megaw L.J. (who later himself became a "culprit" in *Wathes* (*Western*) *Ltd.* v. *Austins* (*Menswear*) *Ltd.*[52]) in *Maredelanto Compania*

Naviera S.A. v. *Bergbau-Handel G.m.b.H.*[53] talking of a possible repudiatory breach in the charterparty:

" ... One of the essential elements of law is some measure of uniformity. One of the important elements of the law is predictability. At any rate in commercial law, there are obvious and substantial advantages in having, where possible, a firm and definite rule for a particular class of legal relationship ... It is surely much better, both for ship-owners and charterers (and, incidentally, for their advisers) when a contractual obligation of this nature is under consideration, and still more when they are faced with the necessity for an urgent decision as to the effects of a suspected breach of it, to be able to say categorically: 'If a breach is proved then the charterer can put an end to the contract,' rather than they should be left to ponder whether or not the courts would be likely, in the particular case, when the evidence has been heard, to decide that in the particular circumstances the breach was or was not such as to go to the root of the contract."

J. *Survival of the Substantive Rule*

There is one point at which the substantive rule of law relating to fundamental breach survives the *Suisse Atlantique* case and this is a notable point of difference between an ordinary repudiatory breach, sometimes termed a breach of condition, and a fundamental breach. Although they both have the same effect, *i.e.* they permit the victim of the breach his option to affirm or repudiate, it would seem that it is perfectly possible to exclude the right to repudiate altogether, for example by means of a clause providing that all breaches of the contractual obligations are to be treated as breaches of warranty and not as a ground for rejecting performance and treating the contract as repudiated. If such a clause is contained in a standard form contract or in a consumer contract, or if the breach is of a term implied by sections 13 to 15 of the Sale of Goods Act 1893 into a non-consumer sale, or of a similar term in a contract of hire-purchase or the related contracts, such as work and materials, under which goods pass, it will be subject to the test of reasonableness under the Unfair Contract Terms Act.[54] If the breach is of a similar implied term in a consumer contract, the clause will be void. But, provided the breach or the contract, as the case may be, is not of this type, or the clause satisfies the requirement of reasonableness, where appropriate, such a clause would be effective. However, it would appear to be a ready inference from some of the speeches in the *Suisse Atlantique* case[55] that the option to repudiate or affirm can never be removed by an exemption clause, however widely but precisely drafted. In other words the exclusion clause may bite, if at all, after the innocent party has exercised his option to affirm and, by virtue of section 9(1) of the Unfair Contract Terms Act 1977, it *may* also bite if he repudiates. It cannot, however, as a matter of law, operate on the option or election itself.

This proposition might appear to be controverted by Donaldson J. in *Kenyon Son & Craven Ltd.* v. *Baxter Hoare & Co. Ltd.*[56] He observes:

> "In all other cases [*i.e.* where there has not been a total failure of consideration] it is a problem of construction whether the exception clauses apply to the breach which has occurred and whether the breach, viewed in the light of all the terms of the contract, is or is not one which gives the innocent party a right to treat the contract as not being binding upon him after the breach."

If by this Donaldson J. is suggesting that, amongst "all the terms of the contract," the exclusion clause itself can deprive the victim of his right "to treat the contract as not being binding on him," then, sensible and desirable though such an approach to construction undoubtedly is, it is difficult to reconcile it with the *dicta* from the House of Lords in the *Suisse Atlantique* case.[57]

K. *The Burden of Proof*

In *Levison* v. *Patent Steam Carpet Cleaning Co. Ltd.,*[58] Lord Denning M.R. took the view that the problem of who carries the burden of proof in the case of fundamental breach is "a moot point for decision." This question can, of course, have an important practical outcome on the case and there is a paucity of authority directly on the matter. In *Woolmer* v. *Delmer Price Ltd.*[59] McNair J. held that the defendants who, having agreed to store the plaintiff's fur coat "at customer's risk," lost it in some unexplained fashion, carried the burden of proving that the loss was not due to fundamental breach. This view was endorsed by Denning L.J. in *J. Spurling Ltd.* v. *Bradshaw*[60] and received the support of a unanimous Court of Appeal in the *Levison* case. It will be recalled from Chapter 4 that there is a line of authority concerned with shipping law to the effect that if a shipowner makes a prime facie case that the cause of the loss was an excepted peril, the burden is then on the shipper to prove that it was not covered by the exceptions.[61] However, it will also be recalled that these were cases dealing with the burden of proof in the event of an ordinary breach where there is a clause of exclusion, not fundamental breach. Also, it was argued in Chapter 4 that these shipping cases perhaps represented decision based as much on public policy as anything else. In these consumer bailments, on the other hand, where the consequences of the breach cause such loss to the bailor as to be fundamental, it is perhaps reasonable to expect the bailee, the manner of the loss being a matter peculiarly within his knowledge if it is within anybody's, to carry the burden of disproving fundamental breach.

There is, however, one authority that causes some difficulty. In *Hunt and Winterbotham (West of England) Ltd.* v. *B.R.S. (Parcels) Ltd.*[62] goods which had been handed to a carrier for delivery were lost, and it was held that the carrier could rely on a limitation clause without disproving fundamental breach. Sir David Cairns in *Levison* v. *Patent Steam Carpet Cleaning Co.*[63] distinguishes *Hunt's* case from *Woolmer* v. *Delmer Price Ltd.*[64] on two grounds. First, he propounds the distinction put forward in *Hunt's* case itself[65] that the problem concerned a contract of carriage and not of deposit, although he is rightly sceptical about this as a proper ground of distinction. Secondly, he suggests that the matter turns on pleading. In *Hunt's* case fundamental breach was not actually pleaded, and so the general question of who had the burden of proof was therefore left open. The Court of Appeal in *Levison* was thus able to hold that when a fundamental breach is actually pleaded by the owner of the goods, the onus is on the bailee to disprove it.

Lord Denning M.R. clearly did not find such sophistry attractive and chose not to rely on it. Instead he felt the matter to be one of principle which the justice of the case demanded should be decided against the bailee. He is the only party with the means of knowing what happened to the goods. If he cannot come up with some explanation as to how they disappeared, then he must take the consequences. After all, it is his business and that is a risk a business takes. Lord Denning M.R. said[66]:

" ... I am clearly of opinion that, in a contract of bailment, when a bailee seeks to escape liability on the ground that he was not negligent or that he was excused by an exception or limitation clause, then he must show what happened to the goods. He must prove all the circumstances known to him in which the loss or damage occurred. If it appears that they were lost or damaged by a slight breach — not going to the root of the contract — he may be protected by the exemption or limitation clause. But, if he leaves the cause of loss or damage undiscovered and unexplained — then I think he is liable: because it is then quite likely that the goods were stolen by one of his servants; or delivered by a servant to the wrong address; or damaged by reckless or wilful misconduct; all of which the offending servant will conceal and not make known to his employer. Such conduct will be a fundamental breach against which the exemption or limitation clause will not protect him.''

Notes

1   Montrose, 15 Can. B. Rev. 760; Unger, 4 Business L.R.30; Melville (1956) 19 M.L.R. 26; Guest (1961) 77 L.Q.R. 98; Reynolds (1963) 79 L.Q.R. 534; Montrose [1964] C.L.J.60, 254; Devlin [1966] C.L.J. 192; Coote (1967) 40 A.L.J.336; Leigh-Jones and Pickering (1970) 86 L.Q.R.513; (1971) 87 L.Q.R. 515; Weir [1970] C.L.J. 189; Coote [1970] C.L.J.221; Weir [1970] C.L.J.189; Baker (1970) 33 M.L.R. 441; Reynolds in *Benjamin's Sale of Goods* (1974), p.440 *et seq.*; Dawson (1975) 91 L.Q.R.380; Coote (1975) 125 N.L.J. 752; Coote (1977) 40 M.L.R.31.

2   (1834) 4 M. & W.399, 404; Professor Coote has called this "a quite unhistorical reliance" (see 40 A.L.J. 336 at p.338) but nevertheless, although Lord Abinger may not have had in mind breach of a fundamental term, he was clearly expressing the view that performance in a totally different way from that contemplated by the contract could not be referrable to the obligation undertaken.

3   [1953] 1 W.L.R. 1468.

4   At p.1470.

5   Atiyah, *Sale of Goods* (1st ed., 1957), pp.81-84; Cheshire and Fifoot, *The Law of Contract* (4th ed., 1956), pp.104-5; *Sutton & Shannon on Contracts* (5th ed. by K.W. Wedderburn), pp.306-307; Guest, (1961) 77 L.Q.R. 98; *cf* Hudson (1957) 20 M.L.R.236 and (1961) 24 M.L.R. 690; Samek (1959) 33 A.L.J. 392 and (1961) 35 A.L.J. 437; Reynolds (1963) 79 L.Q.R.534; Coote, *Exception Clauses,* pp.61-69; Macleod, *Sale and Hire-Purchase,* 56; Coote (1967) 40 A.L.J. 336 at p.337.

6   Curiously, s.12(2) envisages a transaction, called a "contract of sale," which does not appear to fall within the definition of a contract of sale under s.1, since the seller can, under s.12(2), transfer a mere possessory title and not the property in the goods.

7   [1923] 2 K.B. 500; *Karflex Ltd.* v. *Poole* [1933] 2 K.B. 251; *Butterworth* v. *Kingsway Motors Ltd.* [1954] 1 W.L.R.1286.

8   See now Torts (Protection of Goods) Act 1977, s.6.

9   *Andrews* v. *Singer* [1934] 1 K.B. 17.

10   *Hooper* v. *Treffry* (1874) 1 Ex.17; *Wallis, Son & Wells* v. *Pratt & Haynes* [1910] 2 K.B. 1003; *Gurney* v. *Womersley* (1854) 4 E & B 133.

11   See Melville, "The Core of a Contract" (1956) 19 M.L.R. 26.

12   [1923] 1 K.B. 690.

13   At p.697.

14   Coote (1967) 40 A.L.J. 336 at p.338.

15   s.6(2), (3), 13(1).

16   See, *e.g. Unity Finance* v. *Hammond, The Times,* January 12, 1965; in this case the cost of repair to the vehicle was only £14.

17   *Chandler* v. *Webster* [1904] 1 K.B.493; Stoljar (1959) 75 L.Q.R.53.

18   See Stoljar, "The Doctrine of Failure of Consideration" (1959) 75 L.Q.R.53; Goff & Jones, *Law of Restitution,* pp.340-346.

19   Glanville Williams (1941) 57 L.Q.R. 490.

20   *Joseph Thorley Ltd.* v. *Orchis S.S. Co. Ltd.* [1907] 1 K.B.660; *James Morrison & Co. Ltd.* v. *Shaw, Savill & Albion Co. Ltd.* [1916] 2 K.B.783; *Stag Line Ltd.* v. *Foscolo, Mango & Co. Ltd.* [1932] A.C. 328; *L. & N.W. Railway* v. *Neilson* [1922] 2 A.C. 263; *Bontex Knitting Works Ltd.* v. *St. John's Garage* [1943] 2 A11 E.R.690, [1944] 1 A11 E.R.381; *Woolf* v. *Collis Removal Services* [1948] 1 K.B.11; *Davies* v. *Collins* [1945] 1 A11 E.R.247; *Garnham, Harris & Elton Ltd.* v. *Alfred W. Ellis (Transport) Ltd.* [1967] 1 W.L.R.940.

21   *Rugg* v. *Minett* (1809) 11 East 210.

22   *Chanter* v. *Leese* (1839) 5 M. & W. 698, 702; Glanville Williams (1941) 57 L.Q.R. 490 at p.492.

23   *Yeoman Credit* v. *Apps.* [1962] 2 Q.B.508; Glanville Williams, *Law Reform (Frustrated Contracts) Act 1943,* pp.12 and 16.

24   [1943] A.C.32 at p.48.

25   Samek (1959) 33 A.L.J. 392, 397. In the case of frustration this rule has been modified by the Law Reform (Frustrated Contracts) Act 1943.

26   *Fibrosa Spolka Akoyjna* v. *Fairburn Lawson Combe Barbour Ltd.* [1943] A.C.32; Glanville Williams, *Law Reform (Frustrated Contracts) Act 1943;* p.14.

27   *The Julia* [1949] A.C.293, *per* Lord Simonds at p.316.

28 *Blackburn Bobbin Co. Ltd.* v. *T.W. Allen & Sons Ltd.* [1918] 2 K.B.467.
29 *Harbutts Plasticine Ltd.* v. *Wayne Tank and Pump Co. Ltd.* [1970] 1 Q.B.447, *per* Widgery L.J. at 472.
30 [1923] 1 K.B. 690 at p.696.
31 *Nicol* v. *Godts* (1854) 10 Ex.191; *Smeaton Hanscomb & Co.* v. *Sassoon I. Setty & Co.* [1953] 1 W.L.R. 1468, 1470; *Karsales* (*Harrow*) *Ltd.* v. *Wallis* [1956] 1 W.L.R.936, *per* Birkett L.J. at p.942 and *per* Parker L.J. at p.943; *Yeoman Credit Ltd.* v. *Apps* [1962] 2 Q.B.508, *per* Holroyd Pearce L.J. at p.520; *Charterhouse Credit Co.* v. *Tolly* [1963] 2 Q.B.683, *per* Donovan L.J. at p.701 and *per* Upjohn L.J. at p.710; *Suisse Atlantique Société d'Armement Maritime S.A.* v. *N.V. Rotterdamsche Kolen Centrale* [1967] 1 A.C.361, *per* Viscount Dilhorne at p.393 and *per* Lord Reid at pp.397-398.
32 [1962] 2 Q.B.508.
33 At p.520.
34 At p.523.
35 (1834) 1 Bing N.C. 370; see also *Jacobs* v. *Revell* [1900] 2 Ch.858; *Re Courcier and Harold* [1923] 1 Ch.565; *Re Weston & Thomas's Contract* [1907] 1 Ch.244.
36 See *The Law Society's Conditions of Sale* (1973 Revision) No.13; also *National Conditions of Sale* (19th ed.), No. 17.
37 [1917] 1 Ch.613 at p.618.
38 Under the Unfair Contract Terms Act 1977, s.3 a party in breach cannot rely on an exclusion clause to avoid liability, or to render a contractual performance substantially different from that which was reasonably expected of him, and cannot, in reliance on the clause render no performance at all, unless the clause satisfies the requirements of reasonableness under the Act: see *post*. This only applies, however, between contracting parties where one is a consumer or one deals on the other's written standard terms of business. The mere fact that the contract is repudiated is not, by itself, sufficient to deprive the clause of effect if, aside from repudiation, it is found to be reasonable (s.9).
39 Which will admit of an exclusion clause: Sale of Goods Act 1893, s.55(4); Unfair Contract Terms Act 1977, s.6(3).
40 For a discussion of this problem see Coote [1970] C.L.J.221, 226-227.
41 See Upjohn L.J. in *Charterhouse Credit Co. Ltd.* v. *Tolly* [1963] 2 Q.B.683 at p.710.
42 The arguments are rehearsed in Coote (1967) 40 A.L.J. 336 at pp.345-346.
43 Baker (1970) 33 M.L.R. 441.
44 [1943] A.C. 32 at p.46.
45 See Chap. 4.

46 *Coggs* v. *Bernard* (1703) 2 Ld.Raym.909; *Houghland* v. *R.R. Low (Luxury Coaches) Ltd.* [1962] 1 Q.B.694.
47 *Meux* v. *G.E. Railway* [1895] 2 Q.B.387.
48 *Lee Cooper* v. *C.H. Jeakins* [1967] 2 Q.B.1.
49 *Joseph Travers & Sons Ltd.* v. *Cooper* [1915] 1 K.B. 73; *Easson* v. *L.N.E. Railway* [1944] 1 K.B. 421; *Hunt & Winterbotham (West of England) Ltd.* v. *B.R.S. (Parcels) Ltd.* [1962] 1 Q.B.617; *Spurling Ltd.* v. *Bradshaw* [1956] 1 W.L.R. 461.
50 *Cheshire* v. *Bailey* [1905] 1 K.B.237; for a most illuminating discussion of the law and practice relating to dealings with common carriers, see Gorton, *The Concept of the Common Carrier in Anglo-American Law,* especially Chaps. 1 and 3.
51 *Gibbon* v. *Paynton* (1796) 4 Burr. 2298.
52 *Clarke* v. *West Ham Corporation* [1909] 2 K.B. 858 at p.877; *Redhead* v. *Midland Railway* (1869) L.R. 4 Q.B.379 at p.382.
53 The position under the Unfair Contract Terms Act 1977 is considered presently.
54 See Coote, *Exception Clauses,* pp.19-36.
55 *Lilley* v. *Doubleday* (1881) 7 Q.B.D.510; *Woolf* v. *Collis Removal Services* [1948] 1 K.B. 11; see also *Woolmer* v. *Delmer Price* [1955] 1 Q.B.291; *Levison* v. *Patent Steam Carpet Cleaning Co. Ltd.* [1977] 3 W.L.R. 90, *per* Sir David Cairns at p.100.
56 See *Sze Hai Tong Bank Ltd.* v. *Rambler Cycle Co. Ltd.* [1959] A.C.576.
57 [1922] 2 A.C.263.
58 At p.273.
59 [1907] 1 K.B.660; see also *James Morrison & Co. Ltd.* v. *Shaw Savill & Albion Co. Ltd.* [1916] 2 K.B. 783; *Stag Line Ltd.* v. *Foscolo, Mango & Co. Ltd.* [1932] A.C.328.
60 At p.669; see also *Cunard* v. *Buerger* [1927] A.C.1,8.
61 See, *e.g.* Coote, *Exception Clauses,* pp.19-36, 108-116; Treitel, *The Law of Contract* (4th ed.), pp.146-148.
62 See Gorton, *The Concept of the Common Carrier in Anglo-American Law,* Chap.3, para.7.
63 See the cases already cited and also: *Davies* v. *Garrett* (1830) 6 Bing 716; *Scaramanga* v. *Stamp* (1880) 5 C.P.D. 245; *Leduc* v. *Ward* (1888) 20 Q.B.D.475; *Balian* v. *Joly* (1890) 6 T.L.R.345; *The Dunbeth* [1897] P.133; *International Guano* v. *Macandrew* [1909] 2 K.B. 360; *U.S. Shipping Board* v. *Masters* (1922) 10 LL.L.R.573 at p.575. The view that deviation automatically terminates the contract of carriage is first articulated in *Balian* v. *Joly ante,* but was applied with the utmost rigour some 25 years later in *U.S. Shipping Board* v. *Bunge & Born* (1925) 42 T.L.R. 174 where the effect of a

deviation was to disentitle the shipowner from relying on the demurrage provisions of his contract.

64 See, *e.g. Hain* v. *Tate & Lyle* (1936) 41 Com.Cas. 350.

65 *G.H. Renton & Co. Ltd.* v. *Palmyra Trading Corporation of Panama* [1957] A.C.149.

66 *A.F. Colverd & Co. Ltd.* v. *Anglo-Overseas Transport Co. Ltd.* [1961] 2 Lloyd's Rep.352.

67 *The Cap Palos* [1921] P.458.

68 *Thomas National Transport (Melbourne) Pty. Ltd.* v. *May & Baker (Australia) Ltd.* [1966] 2 Lloyd's Rep. 347.

69 *Bontex Knitting Works Ltd.* v. *St. John's Garage* [1943] 2 All E.R.690; affd. [1944] 1 All E.R.381n.

70 [1921] 2 K.B.426.

71 [1967] 1 A.C. 361 at p.412.

72 [1945] 1 All E.R.247.

73 See Chap. 3.

74 See Chap. 4.

75 [1976] 1 Lloyd's Rep. 14 at p.19.

76 The words in quotation marks at the end of the passage come from the judgment of Diplock L.J. in *Hong Kong Fir Shipping Co. Ltd.* v. *Kawasaki Kisen Kaisha Ltd.* [1962] 2 Q.B.26 at pp.72 and 70 respectively.

77 (1936) 41 Com.Cas.350.

78 See *Heyman* v. *Darwins* [1942] A.C.356.

79 (1936) 41 Com.Cas.350, at pp.357 and 362 respectively.

80 [1951] 1 K.B. 240.

81 [1936] 2 All E.R.597.

82 [1951] 2 K.B.882.

83 At pp.889-890.

84 [1953] 1 W.L.R. 1026.

85 At p.1031.

86 [1956] 1 W.L.R. 936.

87 At p.942: " ... a car that would not go was not a car at all."

88 At p.943: " ... the vehicle delivered in effect is not properly described ... as a motor vehicle."

89 At p.940.

90 *Ibid.* italics supplied.

91 *Hain* v. *Tate & Lyle* [1936] 2 All E.R.597.

92 [1963] 2 Q.B.683.

93 [1936] 2 All E.R.597.

94 [1963] 2 Q.B.683.

95 [1967] 1 A.C.361.

96 *Ethel Radcliffe Steamship Co.* v. *Barnett* (1926) 24 Lloyd's L.R.227; *Inverkipp Steamship Co. Ltd.* v. *Bunge & Co.* [1917] 2 K.B.193.

97 [1963] 2 Q.B.683.

98 [1964] 1 Lloyd's Rep. 446 at p.453.

99 [1967] 1 A.C.361 at pp.393, 406, 413, 427, 434.

1 *Ibid.* at p.398.

2 *Ibid.* at p.427.

3 *Ibid.* at p.432.

4 See Coote [1970] C.L.J. 221.

5 *Harbutts Plasticine Ltd.* v. *Wayne Tank and Pump Co. Ltd.* [1970] 1 Q.B.447; *Wathes (Western) Ltd.* v. *Austins (Menswear) Ltd.* [1976] 1 Lloyd's Rep. 14; *Levison* v. *Patent Steam Carpet Cleaning Co. Ltd.* [1977] 3 W.L.R. 90.

6 At p.398.

7 See *United Fresh Meat Co. Ltd.* v. *Charterhouse Cold Storage Ltd.* [1974] 2 Lloyd's Rep. 286; *Levison* v. *Patent Steam Carpet Cleaning Co. Ltd.* [1977] 3 W.L.R. 90, *per* Lord Denning M.R. at p.97.

8 [1976] 1 Lloyd's Rep. 14; see also Reynolds, (1976) 92 L.Q.R.172.

9 At pp.21-22 and 25 respectively.

10 [1971] 1 W.L.R. 519. See also *Wathes (Western) Ltd.* v. *Austins (Menswear) Ltd.* [1976] 1 Lloyd's Rep.14: "I should not wish it to be thought that anything I say in this judgment is indicative of a view, one way or the other, whether the words of the exclusion clause, properly construed, would provide a defence to the whole or any particular part of the counterclaim, on the assumption that the plaintiffs' breach of contract did not achieve the status of a fundamental breach," *per* Megaw L.J. at p.18.

11 Significantly, were the case to fall to be decided under the provisions of the Unfair Contract Terms Act 1977 the clause, to be effective in its protection of the defendants, would, by virtue of s.2(2), have to satisfy the criteria of reasonableness.

12 At p.532.

13 *Trade and Transport Inc.* v. *Iino Kaiun Kaisha Ltd.* [1973] 1 W.L.R. 210; *Harbutts Plasticine Ltd.* v. *Wayne Tank & Pump Co. Ltd.* [1970] 1 Q.B.447, *per* Widgery L.J. at p.472.

14 [1967] 1 A.C.361 at p.426.

15 This does not, however, seem to apply to other, less serious breaches. Although commercial law knows no doctrine of constructive notice — see *Manchester Trust* v. *Furness* [1895] 2 Q.B.539, 545, and *Greer* v. *Downs Supply Co.* [1927] 2 K.B.28, 36 — full knowledge of the breach does not seem to be necessary for the purposes of waiver, in the sense of election of remedies, where the breach is not fundamental: *Panchaud Frères S.A.* v. *Etablissements General Grain Co.* [1970] 1 Lloyd's Rep. 53; see Dugdale and

Yates, "Variation, Waiver and Estoppel — A Re-appraisal" (1976) 39 M.L.R. 680 at pp.687-691.

16 [1970] 1 Q.B.447.

17 At pp.462, 464.

18 At pp.470 and 474 respectively.

19 *Ante*, p. 153.

20 See *Wathes (Western) Ltd.* v. *Austins (Menswear) Ltd.* [1976] 1 Lloyd's Rep.14, *per* Megaw L.J. at pp.15 and 18, Stephenson L.J. at p.23.

21 *Taylor* v. *Caldwell* (1853) 3 B. & S. 826.

22 [1970] 1 W.L.R. 1053; see also *Kenyon Son & Craven Ltd.* v. *Baxter Hoare & Co. Ltd.* [1971] 1 W.L.R. 519, per Donaldson J. at p.531.

23 This reasoning was expressly approved by Megaw L.J. in *Wathes (Western) Ltd.* v. *Austins (Menswear) Ltd.* [1976] 1 Lloyd's Rep. 14 at p.19.

24 [1970] 1 Q.B.447.

25 [1967] 1 A.C. 361 at p.398.

26 Although some support may be derived for it from the decision of the House of Lords in *Moschi* v. *LEP Air Services* [1973] A.C.331, where it was held that where a contract was repudiated for fundamental breach, the liability of the guarantor to cover the debts of the party in breach only related to the damages that could be awarded in respect of obligations broken up to the time of repudiation. The guarantee did not survive to cover losses that were occasioned by the consequent failure to meet future performances. *Cf. Maredelanto Compania Naviera S.A.* v. *Bergbau-Handel GmbH* [1971] 1 Q.B.164 where the Court of Appeal took the view that when a contract came to an end in the event of anticipatory breach on the acceptance of the repudiation, damages were to be assessed on the basis that the wrongdoer would inevitably have taken advantage of the *subsequent* right to terminate the contract: see Coote (1977) 40 M.L.R.31, pp.32-34.

27 [1976] 1 Lloyd's Rep. 14 at pp.17-19.

28 (1933) 48 C.L.R. 457 at pp.476-477. See also Albery (1975) 91 L.Q.R. 337; Gummow (1976) 92 L.Q.R.5.

29 (1936) 41 Com.Cas.350.

30 s.3(2).

31 *Cf.* Consumer Credit Act 1974, s.138.

32 s.4.

33 s.6.

34 s.7.

35 For example a case such as *Wathes (Western) Ltd.* v. *Austins (Menswear) Ltd.* [1976] 1 Lloyd's Rep.14.

36 Treitel, *The Law of Contract* (4th ed.), pp.155-156.

37 See *Suisse Atlantique* [1967] 1 A.C.361 at pp.393, 406, 413, 427, 434.

38   *Levison* v. *Patent Steam Carpet Cleaning Co. Ltd.* [1977] 3 W.L.R. 90 at p.95.

39   [1963] 2 Q.B. 683.

40   [1970] 1 W.L.R.1053.

41   [1967] 2 Lloyd's Rep. 61 at p.67.

42   *Harbutts Plasticine Ltd.* v. *Wayne Tank & Pump Co. Ltd.* [1970] 1 Q.B.447 at p.467; *Mendelssohn* v. *Normand Ltd.* [1970] 1 Q.B.177 at p.184; *United Fresh Meat Co. Ltd.* v. *Charterhouse Cold Storage Ltd.* [1974] 2 Lloyd's Rep. 286; *Levison* v. *Patent Steam Carpet Cleaning Co. Ltd.* [1977] 3 W.L.R. 90 at p.97.

43   [1976] 1 Lloyd's Rep. 14.

44   *Ibid.* at p.21.

45   [1970] 1 Q.B.447.

46   [1976] 1 Lloyd's Rep. 14, *per* Megaw L.J. at pp.17 and 19, *per* Stephenson L.J. at p.23, *per* Sir John Pennycuick at p.24.

47   [1962] 2 Q.B.26 at pp.65-69; see also *Maredelanto Compania Naviera S.A.* v. *Bergbau-Handel GmbH* [1971] 1 Q.B.164; Horton Rogers (1971) 34 M.L.R.190; Greig (1973) 89 L.Q.R.93.

48   *Wickman Ltd.* v. *Schuler A.G.* [1974] A.C.235; Baker [1973] C.L.J.196; Brownsword (1974) 37 M.L.R. 104. See Treitel, *The Law of Contract* (4th ed.), pp.537-552; Reynolds (1963) 79 L.Q.R. 534; *Cehave N.V.* v. *Bremer Handel-gesellschaft mbH* [1976] Q.B.44; Reynolds (1976) 92 L.Q.R.17.

49   At p.472.

50   See the trenchant comments of Schofield in [1970] J.B.L. 145-149. See also Garrett, "The Approach to Law Reform" (1964) 61 *Law Society Gazette* 541.

51   *Christy* v. *Row* (1808) 1 Taunt.300; Sale of Goods Act 1893, s.11(1)(*c*); *Panchaud Frères S.A.* v. *Etablissements General Grain Co.* [1970] 1 Lloyd's Rep.53.

52   [1976] 1 Lloyd's Rep.14.

53   [1971] 1 Q.B.164 at p.205.

54   ss.3, 6 and 7.

55   [1967] 1 A.C.361, notably Lords Reid, Wilberforce and Upjohn.

56   [1971] 1 W.L.R. 519 at p.531.

57   [1967] 1 A.C.361, *per* Viscount Dilhorne at p.395, *per* Lord Reid at p.398, *per* Lord Upjohn at p.419 and *per* Lord Wilberforce at p.432.

58   [1977] 3 W.L.R. 90 at pp.97-98.

59   [1955] 1 Q.B.291.

60   [1956] 1 W.L.R.461, 466.

61   *The Glendarroch* [1894] P.226; *Munro, Brice & Co.* v. *War ⁓Risks Association Ltd.* [1918] 2 K.B.78; *Joseph Constantine Steamship Line Ltd.* v. *Imperial Smelting Corporation Ltd.* [1942] A.C.154 (this last case is

actually on the burden of proof in the event of frustration, but the problem is analagous).

62   [1962] 1 Q.B.617.
63   [1977] 3 W.L.R.90 at p.100.
64   [1955] 1 Q.B.291.
65   [1962] 1 Q.B.617 at p.629.
66   [1977] 3 W.L.R. 90 at p.98.

Chapter 7

CONCLUSION

A. *Interpretation*

The present unmanageably complex state of the law relating to exclusion clauses, particularly in relation to the doctrines of fundamental breach and breach of a fundamental term, stems essentially from one problem. With woefully few exceptions, which have been discussed above in Chapter 4[1] an exclusion clause is disregarded in determining what the parties have agreed shall be their rights and obligations under the agreement. It is only when such rights and obligations have been ascertained that the exclusion clause will be looked at. The exclusion clause will then be treated as a completely separate entity, raising such questions as whether it is a part of the rest of the contract at all; whether, on its construction, it can operate to bar a claim based on breach of the obligations already ascertained; whether, where breach of a fundamental term is alleged, there are primary obligations or core duties arising from the relationship created by the contract, regardless of the contract's specific terms,[2] and so on.

In Chapter 4 the fallacy and difficulties inherent in such an approach were discussed and it was suggested that, so far as the construction of the contract is concerned, an exclusion clause should be treated no differently from the rest of the terms. It delimits rights, or prevents them from arising, in precisely the same way as the positively worded clauses do.

Viewed in this way, an exclusion clause is simply one group of words which, when taken along with all the other words which make up the contract, is subjected to certain interpretative processes. Since not all the statements made during negotiations give rise to liability, the court must first ascertain whether the parties intended to create obligations by what they said and wrote, *i.e.* whether the statements become terms of the contract. This process is exactly the same whether the words to be examined are framed negatively, in the form of an exclusion, or positively, in the form of an undertaking. If an exclusion clause is worded in such a way as to prevent a right accruing to the other party, such as an exclusion of warranty clause, then it should be reasonably clear that any statement made by the promisor which, aside from the exclusion, would be regarded as a warranty was not, in the circumstances, intended by the parties to be anything than, at most, a mere representation. Doctrines of fundamental breach or breach of a fundamental term would have no place in this scheme. There will be no terms or consequences liability for which cannot be excluded at all, or cannot be excluded save subject to special rules. If, having determined what contractual force to give to the words the parties use, including the exclusion clause, the court decides that, despite the clause, the promisor is still in breach, this would not be because of any rule of law or principle of construction that prevented the exclusion clause from applying to the breach, but simply because the court has found that, in the light of all the terms, the promisor agreed to perform the obligation which it is alleged he has not performed. If the court were to find for the promisor, again this would not be because the exclusion clause by itself operates as a defence to the claim, but because the promisor never gave the undertaking in the first place which it is alleged he has broken.

B. *The Consumer Interest*

It has, it is hoped, been demonstrated through these pages that the trend of the last 25 years or so, in both court and legislature, has been for the promotion and protection of what was, in Chapter 1, characterised as "the consumer interest." Certainly since the Molony Report of 1962[3] most of the legislative effort in the field of commercial law has been directed towards consumer protection. Several of the business interests consulted for the survey discussed in Chapter 1 expressed the view that commercial operators were receiving the backwash of legislation not specifically designed for them or their needs. The new approach to contractual interpretation discussed above is dependent solely upon the common law. It would be unrealistic to suppose, however, in the present climate and in the light of the developing pattern over the years since the Second World War, that were the law now to return to the common law principles described earlier in this Chapter, it would remain that way for long.

Certainly it is possible to frame an argument for the preservation of freedom of contract. On utilitarian grounds one could argue that since the law of tort protects the interests of strangers to the agreement, enforcement of that agreement will tend to maximise the welfare of the parties to it and therefore the good of society as a whole. Such a view shifts the problem of protection from the law of contract to the law of tort. The crucial question for tort law then becomes one of the scope and identification of the "interests" to be protected. On the one hand, they could be defined so as to include the expectation of profit from trade, in which case all economic harm would fall within the scope of the law of tort. On the other hand, they could cover the exclusive use and possession of one's person and property, in which case most forms of economic harm would fall, as is at present the case, outside the protection of tort law.[4] On libertarian grounds, also, it is clear that one of the functions of the law is to guarantee to individuals a sphere of influence in which they will be able to operate without having to justify themselves to the state or to third parties. If one individual is entitled to do, within the limits of the law of tort, what he pleases with what he owns, then two individuals who operate with those same constraints should have the same right with respect to their mutual affairs against the rest of the world.

Whilst such arguments may still hold good with regard to the commercial world, they cannot really be supported in the field of consumer protection. By consumer is here meant one who acquires goods or services for private use or consumption. There are others such as small shopkeepers, boarding house proprietors, certain professional persons, who acquire supplies and equipment for business use on so limited a scale and with so limited a business experience and resources that it might be thought their problems were closely comparable with those of the domestic consumer. However, the problems experienced by the small business may differ in scale from those encountered by the larger concerns, but they all form part of the pattern of commercial relationship arising between those who have elected to buy and sell as a matter of business. As such, they must be set apart from the problems of the domestic customer, who shops purely in a private capacity.[5] For similar reasons, there is a considerable difference between dealings in standard or "back-of-order" form in commercial transactions, where, as the survey described in Chapter 1 shows, the view of businessmen is that business efficacy is thereby achieved, and standard form dealings in the consumer field where frequently considerations other than the strictly economic may prevail.

It can hardly be doubted that the consumer, as thus defined, is in need of some form of protection. It is difficult for him to recognise the composition and manner of production of goods offered in the modern market because of the development of complicated production techniques. The job of ascertaining and assessing the wide range of alternative choices open to him is more than the consumer can be expected to do. The sale of branded and nationally advertised goods reduces the retailer's function to that of handing over what the customer has already been persuaded to buy before entering the shop; partly for this reason, therefore, and partly because it is in many cases as difficult for the retailer as it is for his customer to sort out the merits and shortcomings of the goods he stocks, the retailer is unable in many cases to give expert advice to the individual customer. In such difficulties the consumer will frequently find it beyond his power to make a wise and informed choice, or may have, in fact, no choice at all, and is thus vulnerable to exploitation and deception, both in relation to the goods or services he received and in relation to the agreements under which they are supplied.

We are here particularly concerned with the agreement or contract under which goods or services are supplied to the consumer. Given the fact that the common law is unable to provide protection in relation to these agreements without straining the principles of contractual interpretation to an illogical degree, the task of protection falls upon legislation. There are already, of course, legislative controls over consumer agreements that create the potential for comprehensive review, notably the Trade Descriptions Act 1968, the Fair Trading Act 1973, Pts. I and II, and the Consumer Credit Act 1974. In the specific area of exclusion clauses, however, recent legislative proposals, in the form of the Supply of Goods (Implied Terms) Act 1973 and the Unfair Contract Terms Act 1977, make exactly the same error that has been identified in the common law. The problems inherent in viewing exclusion clauses apart from the other promises and undertakings in the contract are exactly the same whether that approach be dictated by the common law or by statute. It gives a false view of, and a false emphasis to, the agreement.

The Unfair Contract Terms Act 1977 goes even further and in some cases imposes such an approach on some commercial as well as consumer agreements. This, it is submitted, is unwarranted. As has been shown, this is not popular with the business community. It interferes with legitimate planning of contractual risk, leads to uncertainty, and applies to the commercial world solutions designed for what is essentially a consumer problem.

Given, nevertheless, the need for some consumer protection, and given the undesirability of allowing judicial review of one clause (the exclusion clause) only, it is suggested that the viable alternative is to permit review of the whole agreement. In other words, the courts should interpret the contract as a whole, including the exclusion clause, to ascertain what was agreed, and may then interfere to protect the consumer interest in accordance with a statutory criterion, in the light of the contract as a whole. An example, from a ticket issued by a large chain of retail chemists when films are handed in for processing, is as follows: "Whilst all precautions are normally taken when photographic material is accepted by us, liability for loss or damage, consequential or otherwise, however caused, is limited to the replacement of the materials." Under such a contract the chemist does not promise to process the film and be liable for its safe custody and proper processing with a defence if he does not. He simply gives a statement of aspiration — that he hopes to do his best — but his liability is simply to return the film, or the cost of the material, at his option. A court reviewing such an agreement under our proposed statutory power would not look at the exclusion clause alone, nor would the exclusion clause simply be banned. The whole contract would be subject to review. Given the parties' respective knowledge, bargaining power, etc., the contract might be quite just. It might be just with an abatement of price. It might be an appropriate undertaking to give where the processing work was unusually difficult, or the film an old one that had passed its date limit. Or, alternatively, the contractual undertaking might, in the circumstances, be regarded as unjust and struck down, leaving the problem to be solved by the law of tort of bailment.

C. *Reasonableness or Unconscionability*

The present legislative controls, albeit, it is submitted, directed at too narrow a base, depend upon the test of reasonableness as discussed in Chapter 3. An alternative, already in operation in certain areas of English law[6] and incorporated into the Uniform Commercial Code in the United States[7] is the doctrine of unconscionability.[8] Section 2-302 of the Uniform Commercial Code provides neither a definition of the term "unconscionable" nor an elaboration of the conceptual framework of the doctrine. Instead, the section describes the remedies available to a court once it has found an unconscionable contract or clause. The section requires a hearing to be held before the court determines whether unconscionability is present. In making a decision on unconscionability, the court is required to examine the commercial setting of the individual transaction, thereby prohibiting use of standardised rules. Each case must be judged on its own particular facts. The statutory language does not define the concept, and provides procedures which hinder the development of a rigid definition. The Code provides as follows:

> "(1) If the court as a matter of law finds the contract or any clause of the contract to have been unconscionable at the time it was made the court may refuse to enforce the contract, or it may enforce the remainder of the contract without the unconscionable clause, or it may so limit the application of any unconscionable clause as to avoid any unconscionable result.

(2) When it is claimed or appears to the court that the contract or any clause thereof may be unconscionable the parties shall be afforded a reasonable opportunity to present evidence as to its commercial setting, purpose and effect to aid the court in making the determination.''

Professor Leff[9] distinguishes, in the application of section 2-302, between bargaining aspects of unconscionability, *i.e.* circumstances which militate against free assent, which he terms "procedural" unconscionability and substantive aspects of unconscionability, *i.e.* contracts or contractual terms which appear too heavily weighted in favour of one of the parties.

Taking "procedural" unconscionability first, the section is a tool, in addition to the traditional means of dealing with misleading bargaining conduct, such as fraud, duress, misrepresentation, legal incapacity, etc., for controlling certain types of devices which are used to reach agreement, including the use of standard form, and small print contracts and clauses.[10] It is further useful to redress the balance arising from an inequality of bargaining position where this results in some element of deception or substantive unfairness,[11] although the section cannot be invoked simply on the ground of inequality of bargaining strength where no such unfair advantage is taken.[12] Finally procedural unconscionability has been used to control the exploitation, through contracts, of the underprivileged or inadequate consumer. The great merit of a test of unconscionability here is that the court can take account of the particular inadequacies and susceptibilities of the individual consumer, rather than imposing the standards of the "reasonable" or "average" consumer which a test of reasonableness imports. In *Williams* v. *Walker-Thomas Furniture Co.*[13] the court put the test in this way: "Did each party to the contract, considering his obvious education or lack of it, have a reasonable opportunity to understand the terms of the contract ... ?"

The main focus of section 2-302 is, however, on issues sub-sumed under the general heading of "substantive" uncon-scionability, a classification that seeks to distinguish ques-tions of unfair content from those relating to bargaining misconduct. A court is enabled to apply the section so as to characterise a whole agreement unconscionable where one party has driven too hard a bargain producing an overall imbalance in favour of one party.[14] It can also, of course, characterise particular clauses, such as exemption clauses, price clauses, limitations on available remedies, repossession clauses in credit contracts and so on, as unconscionable. The court will react by striking down the whole contract, striking down particular clauses and even rewriting the agreement where appropriate. Unconscionability can be used as a straight defence to resist an action for damages or a claim of specific performance.

It is a provision such as that found in section 2-302, but limited to consumer agreements, that could be adapted for use in English contract law. The concept of unconscionability has two advantages over the present concept of reasonable-ness, with which it is frequently confused.[15] The essential difference seems to lie in the fact that notions of conscience and of unconscionability are essentially subjective. Tests of reasonableness are objective, determined in accordance with the conduct, thoughts and responses one might expect from the reasonable man.[16] As many American jurisdictions have discovered, the consumer may not be "a reasonable man" in the objective sense. He may be illiterate, he may not speak or read English, he may not have the education, under-standing or expertise to contract without being taken advant-age of and, of course, his bargaining position may be inferior. A test of unconscionability can cater for the susceptibilities of the particular parties to the agreement in a way that the more objective criterion of reasonableness does not.

Also, by having regard to a test of conscience, the court can have regard to the conduct of both parties, not just the party against whom relief is sought. It may be, for instance, that the consumer, not himself having shown honesty and fair dealing, should not receive the relief he seeks. Such factors are subsumed in a test of unconscionability but not in reasonableness, the effects of which appear, in any event, to be exhausted when the contract is made. Conduct after the making of the agreement does not seem to play any part in the test of reasonableness.

An unconscionability doctrine should, in the consumer field, inhibit the supplier from automatically asserting all conceivable rights in all transactions and for this reason precise and exact definition is unnecessary. Indeed, if exact definition were possible, the draftsmen of standard form consumer agreements could draft to the threshold of unconscionability, recreating the situation which is, in essence, current today. The doctrine will not, of course, be completely unlimited. A case-law gloss would quickly build up round the bare statutory words, establishing limitations on the doctrine. The matter may be summed up in the words of the Official Comment to section 2-302 of the Uniform Commercial Code. It states: "The principle is one of the prevention of oppression and unfair surprise ... and not of disturbance of allocation of risks because of superior bargaining power."[17]

Notes

1 See pp. 74-79, *ante.*
2 See Meyer, "Contracts of Adhesion and the Doctrine of Fundamental Breach," 50 Va. L.Rev. 1178 (1964).
3 Final Report of the Committee on Consumer Protection, Cmnd. 1781 (1962).

4 See Epstein, "Intentional Harms," 4 *Journal of Legal Studies* 391 (1975).

5 Final Report of the Committee on Consumer Protection (*Molony Report*), Cmnd. 1781 (1962), Pt. 1.

6 See Waddams, "Unconscionability in Contracts" (1976) 39 M.L.R. 369.

7 Except in California and North Carolina.

8 See Ellinghaus, "In Defense of Unconscionability," 78 Yale L.J. 757 (1969); Leff, "Unconscionability and the Code — The Emperor's New Clause," 115 U.Pa.L.Rev. 485 (1967); Braucher, "The Unconscionable Contract or Term," 31 U.Pitt.L.Rev.337 (1969); Leff, "Unconscionability and the Crowd — Consumers and the Common Law Tradition," 31 U.Pitt.L. Rev.349 (1969); Murray, "Unconscionability," 31 U.Pitt.L.Rev.1 (1969); Spagnole, "Analyzing Unconscionability Problems," 117 U.Pa.L.Rev. 931 (1969); Epstein, "Unconscionability: A Critical Re-appraisal," *Journal of Law and Economics* 293 (1975).

9 115 U.Pa.L.Rev. 485.

10 *David* v. *Manufacturers Hanover Trust Co.* 4 U.C.C. R. S. 1145 (N.Y. Civ. Ct. 1968); *Zabriskie Chevrolet Inc.* v. *Smith*, 99 N.J. Super. 441, 240 A. 2d. 195 (1968). *cf. American Home Improvement Inc.* v. *MacIver*, 105 N.H. 435, 201 A.2d 886 (1964).

11 *Paragon Homes of Midwest, Inc.* v. *Crace* 4 U.C.C. R.S. 19 (N.Y. Sup.Ct. 1967); *Paragon Homes of New England, Inc.* v. *Langlois* 4 U.C.C. R.S.16 (N.Y. Sup.Ct. 1967).

12 *Sinkoff Beverage Co.* v. *Jos. Schlitz Brewing Co.* 51 Misc. 2d 446, 448, 273 N.Y.S. 2d 364, 366 (1966).

13 350 F.2d 445 (D.C. Cir.) (1965) at 449; see also *State by Lefkowitz* v. *ITM Inc.* 52 Misc.2d 39, 275 N.Y.S. 2d 303 (1966); *Frostifresh Corp.* v. *Reynoso* 52 Misc.2d 26, 274, N.Y.S. 2d 757 (1966), rev'd with respect to *quantum*, 54 Misc.2d 119, 281, N.Y.S. 2d 964 (1967).

14 See *Campbell Soup Co.* v. *Wentz* 172 F.2d 80 (3d Cir. 1948) at 83-84.

15 See, *e.g.* Waddams, "Unconscionability in Contracts" (1976) 39 M.L.R. 369.

16 See dicta of Lord Denning M.R. in *Gillespie Bros. & Co. Ltd.* v. *Roy Bowles Transport Ltd.* [1973] Q.B. 400 at p.416, and *Levison* v. *Patent Steam Carpet Cleaning Co. Ltd.* [1977] 3 W.L.R. 90 at p.95.

17 U.C.C. § 2-302, Comment 1.

INDEX